How to Set Up a CIC & Get Funded

How to Set Up a CIC & Get Funded

A Complete Guide to Community Interest Companies

Kexx

First published in Great Britain in 2026
by Authors & Co.
www.authorsandco.pub

ISBN 978-1-917623-39-1 (paperback)

ISBN 978-1-917623-40-7 (hardback)

Contents

Introduction

You probably have an excellent reason for picking up this book. Maybe an idea has been sitting quietly at the back of your mind for months, even years. Maybe you've lived through something that changed how you see the world, and now you're wondering if you could turn that experience into something that helps others. Or maybe you've simply reached a point where you know there must be more purpose to life and work than what you're doing right now can offer you.

Whatever brought you here, you're in exactly the right place.

This book is for people who feel that pull to make a difference but don't yet know how. People who see a gap that nobody else seems to be filling. People who care deeply, think differently, and believe community still matters.

This is not a business book in the traditional sense; it's a book about impact, belief, and building something meaningful that also pays the bills. It is for people who don't fit neatly into one world – not fully corporate, not quite charitable – and are determined to create something powerful and lasting. A Community Interest Company makes that possible.

The world feels uncertain right now. Budgets are shrinking, public services are stretched, and people are searching for meaning as much as stability. In that world, Community Interest Companies matter deeply. They fill the gaps left by traditional systems and bring creativity, compassion and lived experience into spaces that often feel cold or bureaucratic. They create jobs, rebuild connections and give ordinary people a way to act on the issues that frustrate them most.

CICs prove that business can have heart and that doing good can be good business. They don't just change lives; they reshape how society works from the ground up.

When I started my first CIC, there was almost no information out there. I had no mentor or map. I learned the hard way, through late nights, failed applications, and a fair amount of trial and error. Over the years, I've helped thousands of founders set up their own CICs. Every one of them came to me with the same mix of excitement and fear. They weren't business people in suits. They were mothers, teachers, youth workers, artists, carers, musicians: people with lived experience of hardship who had the spark of an idea and the courage to act on it.

They didn't want to make millions. They wanted to make meaning.

But the hard, unfortunate truth is that good intentions aren't enough. Passion is the spark, but structure is the oxygen. Without structure, ideas stay small. Without funding, you burn out. Without clarity, the world never sees what you can do. This book exists to stop that from happening. It shows you it's possible to build something with heart that also works in practice, something that changes lives while giving you the stability you need to keep going.

If you've ever thought, "I'd love to help, but I don't know where to start... I'm not a business person," this book is for you. If you feel that mix of fear and excitement when you imagine doing something on your own terms, you're exactly who I wrote this for.

You don't need a degree in business or a background in finance. You don't need permission. You just need willingness, persistence and the right foundation. I have worked with people who started from nothing: single parents, people on benefits, people who were told they weren't professional enough, and I've watched them go on to raise hundreds of thousands of pounds, create jobs and transform lives. They didn't achieve this by being lucky. They achieved it by learning how to build structure around their purpose. This book will help you do that, too.

You won't find corporate jargon, get-rich-quick promises or complicated financial formulas here. You won't be told to become someone else in order to succeed. You will find real stories, real strategies and real mistakes... others' and my own. You will see exactly how to turn your idea into a funded, functional, fulfilling organisation that does good and survives doing it.

There will be moments when I tell you things you might not want to hear. Some things take longer than you expect. Some projects fail. Some people won't understand what you're trying to do. That is all part of it. Every founder feels that frustration at the start. What matters is that you keep going.

This book will give you the tools, confidence and mindset to turn your idea into a real, working organisation. But more than that, it will give you permission to take your own story seriously. Permission to value your skills. To believe you're capable of building something bigger than yourself.

You will learn the practical side: how to register, apply for funding, manage money and stay compliant. You will also learn the emotional side: how to handle rejection, overcome self-doubt and stay connected to your mission when the work feels heavy. By the end, you'll have more than a CIC. You will have clarity about who you are, what you stand for, and what you want to build in the world.

You don't need to rush through this book. Take your time. Reflect after each chapter. Use a notebook. Scribble ideas. Write down the communities or causes you care about. You will be amazed at how quickly your vision starts to take shape once you see it written down. And if you're already running a CIC, use this book to refine what you've built. Strengthen it. Simplify it. Align it with the person you've become.

There is no single path through this work. There are as many versions of success as there are people reading this. But there is one constant truth. Every great CIC begins with someone deciding to act.

You can be that someone.

The chapters ahead will take you from possibility to action. First, you'll see what CICs can do through the real stories of people who've built them. Then you'll learn the structure, funding, branding, contracts and sustainability skills that will help you create your own. By the final chapter, you'll see that this isn't just about setting up an organisation. It is about setting yourself free – from doubt, from confusion and from the limits you thought were permanent.

This isn't theory. It is a guide written by someone who's done it, made the mistakes and come out the other side determined to help others do it better.

So take a deep breath. Grab a pen. Open your mind.

Your next chapter, the one where your idea becomes real, starts right here.

Reflection:

Take a quiet moment before diving in. You might want a notebook or a digital space where you can record your thoughts as you move through the book. These are questions to ground you before you start building.

- Why did you pick up this book today?
- What has drawn you towards purpose-led work or community change?
- Which part of your own story do you think might hold the seed of your mission?
- How do you want to feel at the end of this journey? Confident? Clear? Connected?

Exercise:

Write a short paragraph that begins with: "I want to make a difference by…"

Don't overthink it. Let the words spill out. This will be your first glimpse of your 'why'.

1

The Impact of CICs and the People Who Run Them

If you have ever felt pulled to do something meaningful but did not know where to start, Community Interest Companies are one of the UK's best-kept secrets: a way to build a business that serves people as much as it sustains you.

You are about to see what that looks like in real life. This first chapter is about possibility – ordinary people who have turned lived experience into impact, purpose into structure, and ideas into action.

Community Interest Companies change lives. They change the lives of the people they serve and, just as deeply, the lives of the people who create them. A CIC is more than a business. It is a structure built for purpose: for people who want to make a difference and still make a living. It gives shape to an idea that otherwise might stay small, something that begins with one person's experience and grows into genuine community impact.

That is why so many founders are drawn to this world. They are not typical entrepreneurs chasing profit for profit's sake. They are people with heart. People who have lived through something difficult, seen the gaps in support, and decided to fill them. Their pain becomes purpose. Their lived experience becomes fuel.

Every month, through CIC Tribe, I meet hundreds of new founders. Each brings a story – often personal, sometimes painful – and a deep desire to do good. Watching what happens next is extraordinary. They arrive unsure, sometimes a little scared, but full of hope. Then they learn how to build structure, apply for funding and turn their ideas into action. Soon, they are running projects, delivering impact and seeing lives change, including their own.

What starts as a small act of courage grows into something much bigger: opportunity, visibility, confidence. It is one thing to say that CICs change lives. It is another to see it happen before your eyes.

Real People, Real Change

Take Natalie, for example. She found me when I had just launched my first course, *How to Set up a CIC and Get Grant Funded in Four Months*. At the time, there was just one video on YouTube and a lot of faith. Natalie was a mother living with multiple sclerosis. Through her own experience, she had seen how people in the Black community were treated differently within the NHS – the lack of understanding, the lack of resources, the quiet inequality of it all. She wanted to change that.

She powered through the course and within six weeks had launched her CIC, *The Nerve of My MS*. I wrote her applications, and she applied for a £10,000 grant from the National Lottery Community Fund and got it. Her project brought together people with MS to share stories, support one another, and educate the wider community. She delivered it beautifully. Pharmaceutical companies took notice. Invitations to speak at international conferences followed. Soon after, she was featured in *Forbes* Magazine.

From frustration to international recognition. That is what happens when an idea finds its structure.

Then there is Hamaz, who turned his passion for cricket into a community powerhouse. After completing my online course, he began applying for grants. He did not stop at one or two. In his first year, he secured sixteen grants totalling £140,000. What changed was not just his ability to apply for funding, but his mindset. He went from hoping someone might help to knowing he could make things happen. His club now runs youth programmes, community events and mentoring schemes. The impact is visible, and the pride is obvious. That is what persistence looks like. That is what belief can build.

And then there is Tracey. She worked for years in the NHS, a solid job with security and a pension, everything society tells us to value. But inside, she knew she wanted to be an artist. When she told a friend, they laughed. "You? But you're not an artist." That might have stopped someone else, but not her. She applied for Arts Council funding, ran her first few community art projects, travelled to Jamaica using its history to inspire her work, and then more. One by one, those projects built her confidence, her portfolio and her career. Eventually, she had exhibitions, academic offers of a PhD, and national recognition. She was no longer NHS Tracey. She was an artist.

These stories might sound extraordinary, but they are not rare. They are the natural result of people being given a structure that supports their purpose. A CIC does not turn people into heroes. It gives them the tools to act on the change they already care about. It brings clarity, credibility and momentum to what might otherwise remain a dream.

This book will give you those tools. Over the coming chapters, I will show you how to build that structure for yourself, to create a CIC that feels true to you, funds itself properly and delivers genuine impact.

If any part of you feels a spark reading this, hold on to it. That spark is where every great CIC begins. You might not have all the answers yet, and that is fine. Nobody does when they start. But as you turn the pages, you will begin to see what is possible, not just for your community but for you.

Is My Idea Right for a CIC?

Most ideas begin half-formed. That is normal. The real question is where your work sits on the spectrum between charity and business. If you only ever want to rely on grants and public fundraising, you may be closer to a charity. If your focus is private profit, dividends and shareholders, you are looking at a limited company. A Community Interest Company sits between the two. It welcomes grant funding and community support, while leaving room to trade, sell services and build income streams that keep the work going.

Once you understand that shape, the next step is simple. Match your idea to the priorities of funders. If you want funding from Sport England, design a project that gets inactive people moving. If you want support from Arts Council England, bring in artists, plan clear creative outcomes, and show how your project serves your community. Read priorities first, then build the project to fit. That approach turns a good intention into a fundable proposal.

You might already be doing something informally. Perhaps you run a support group in a church hall, or you are a business owner who keeps giving away help because you care. That is common. A CIC gives that work a safe home. It protects your liability, formalises what you are already doing, and opens the door to grant funding so you can stop paying for everything yourself. Many people in our communities are doing brilliant things for free. They should not carry that cost forever. Structure makes the work sustainable.

If your idea feels small, that is fine. A CIC can be small. You can keep it as a side project, run one morning a week, and only apply for occasional small grants. Some founders keep a CIC dormant for a year or two and pick it up when the right funding appears. If, however, your plan is simply a small private venture that will be supported by light trading or a simple membership, and you do not intend to apply for grants or demonstrate community benefit, a standard limited company may be a better fit. The goal is not to force your idea into a CIC. It is to choose the structure that truly serves it.

Fear of formalising your structure is natural. Imposter syndrome, unhelpful comments from others, and the weight of paperwork can make people stall. The alternative is worse. Without structure, you carry the risk, pay the costs and limit your reach. With a CIC, you can bring in volunteers, pay people fairly and share the load. The paperwork is front-loaded. Once you get through the setup, life gets easier because the work has a home that can grow.

If you are unsure what to write in your governing statement, keep your community definition broad enough to evolve. Many people make the mistake of writing something so narrow that they later have to amend it. Leave room for growth. Your projects can specialise, but your paperwork should not trap you.

Finally, remember that feeling guilty about funding helps no one. Your time has value. Your skills deserve payment. Being funded to serve your community is not taking money from others. It is what makes the work possible for the long term.

Reflection:

- Have you ever turned your own challenge or hardship into something positive for others?
- What would it mean for you personally to build something that creates lasting change?
- What fears come up when you think about formalising your idea - and what might sit beneath them?
- What would happen if you gave yourself permission to try anyway?

Exercise:

Grab a notebook and write freely for ten minutes.

1. **List three people or groups** who would benefit most from your idea. Picture them clearly – what are they facing right now, and how would your work help?
2. **Describe what would change** in their lives if your CIC existed. Think practically and emotionally. Would they feel safer, more confident, more connected?
3. **Reflect on what drives you.** Why this cause, and why now? What personal experiences have shaped the way you see the problem you want to solve?

When you finish, read your notes back. Notice what stands out, what feels most alive or urgent. That is the heart of your mission. You don't need the structure or the plan yet – just the clarity of why it matters. Everything else will build from there.

2

What Is a Community Interest Company and What Does It Do?

Every great CIC begins the same way: with a scribbled idea in a notebook and a question: *how on earth do I make this real?*

Understanding what a Community Interest Company is gives you that first bit of solid ground beneath your feet. It is the moment when a good intention becomes something fundable, accountable and respected.

Chapter One showed you the heart of this movement; this chapter will show you its bones.

A CIC, or Community Interest Company, is a UK legal structure created in 2005 to give people a way to run a business for community benefit rather than private profit. In other parts of the world, you might hear it called a social enterprise or a not-for-profit organisation. Whatever the label, the goal is the same: to build a business that makes money and makes a difference.

When I started my own CIC in 2012, there was barely any information available. I learned through trial, error and persistence. Now the landscape looks completely different. Social media, online training and communities like CIC Tribe have made it possible for anyone with a cause to find guidance and support.

Through CIC Tribe, I see this transformation every day. My YouTube channel has over ten thousand subscribers, and every month about one thousand people reach out wanting to learn how to start their own CIC. That number still surprises me. Yet even with that growth, there is room for more.

There are now more than thirty-seven thousand CICs in the UK, with around six hundred new ones registered every month. But that is nowhere near enough. There is still a shortage of strong, well-run community interest companies ready to deliver projects, apply for funding and take up contracts. The demand for social good far outweighs the supply. The opportunity is there, waiting for people willing to step forward.

It is important to recognise that structure can feel intimidating. The word ‘company’ alone can put people off. It sounds corporate, complicated... a world away from community and kindness. But once you understand what a CIC really is, the fear fades. Structure does not box you in, it holds you steady. It turns ideas into something real.

Understanding the Structure

A Community Interest Company sits somewhere between a charity and a private limited company. It combines the social purpose of a charity with the freedom of a business. Like a charity, a CIC can apply for grants and fundraise because it is not set up for private profit. It has an 'asset lock', meaning that any surplus or assets must remain within the organisation and be used to benefit the community. This legal safeguard reassures funders that their money is being used properly.

Unlike most charities, a CIC can also earn income through trading. It can sell products, deliver training, or offer paid-for services alongside its community work. This lets you build something sustainable rather than relying entirely on grants or donations.

A youth CIC might run mentoring programmes funded by local councils while selling sports workshops to schools. A mental health CIC could offer free support groups funded by the NHS while delivering workplace wellbeing training that pays for itself. These are not abstract examples; this kind of balance keeps thousands of small organisations alive and thriving across the UK.

There are two main types of CIC: limited by guarantee and limited by shares.

If your goal is to apply for grants or fundraise publicly, you will want to be limited by guarantee. This type has no shareholders or dividends. Every penny your CIC earns is reinvested in the work you do. You can pay yourself fairly for your role, employ staff and cover your costs, but you cannot take profits out as personal income.

A CIC limited by shares works more like a traditional company. It can issue shares and pay dividends, but it cannot usually access grant funding or public fundraising. If your aim is social impact rather than private profit, limited by guarantee is almost always the right route.

Another vital feature of a CIC is the asset lock. If your company ever closes, any remaining funds or property must be passed to another organisation with similar aims, usually another CIC or a charity. You cannot keep what is left. Many founders list a well-known charity, such as the NSPCC, as their nominated asset-lock body. This safeguard is one of the reasons CICs earn so much trust from funders and partners.

The first time you read about things like asset locks and limited guarantees, it can sound heavy. But once you grasp the purpose, it makes complete sense. These rules exist to protect your mission, not restrict it. They give the structure its credibility. Funders love CICs because they can see that your work is tied to genuine community outcomes, not personal gain.

Here is a big tip that no one else will tell you. Don't put something you designed (like a course or programme) in your CIC because the CIC will own it. Instead, put it in your limited company and license its use to the CIC. Think about it. That is yours: your work, your knowledge. You need to own it, and if it's sellable, you need to be able to earn the profits from it as dividends/shares.

Think of your CIC as your vehicle to get grant funding, fund-raising income and public contracts. Your work/expertise belongs to you/your limited company as a social enterprise licensed or hired to the CIC.

Getting It Right From the Start

Get started with a good name. Check it on Companies House, Google and the trademark register (UK Intellectual Property Office) to check it is available. Do not make it too narrow.

When you first sit down to write your CIC36 Form and Articles of Association, your two formation documents, it can feel like another world of jargon. But that form is the foundation of everything that follows, so it is worth taking the time to get it right.

The form asks who your community is and what activities you plan to deliver. Many people rush this, make the common mistake of being too narrow, and box themselves in without realising it. Or they use AI, which creates nonsense and fluff that will get you rejected for not being clear.

You might think you want to serve exclusively women experiencing menopause, but what if you later want to run a project teaching teenage girls about their periods, or educate men about menopause in the workplace? You need your CIC to allow that flexibility. Keep your definition wide enough to grow into. Always add to the list other groups of people you may work with.

The same goes for geography. It is easier to start broad. If you only list one small town or area, you might need to amend your paperwork later if you want to expand. Think of your community as anyone who could reasonably benefit from what you do.

Another mistake is underplaying the difference your work will make. Companies House want to see a clear community benefit. Many people write about their projects in a soft or understated way, when truthfully, their work changes lives.

If you help a woman manage menopause symptoms, you might prevent a divorce. If you support a young person at risk of exclusion, you could keep them out of prison. If you run mental health workshops, you might prevent someone reaching crisis point. You have to be honest about that impact.

Setting up your CIC correctly is not just about ticking boxes. It is about building something solid that reflects your real intentions. A strong CIC36 tells a story. It says: this is who we help, this is how we help them, and this is the difference it will make. Once you have that clear, you can move forward with confidence. You can change your CIC objectives or name at any time on Companies House, so don't worry, but choosing them well from the start makes things smoother.

Finding Your Mission

Every CIC needs a mission statement, a single line that captures your purpose and intent. It should be clear, active and human. Something like *helping people realise their potential, bringing communities together through creativity,* or *supporting wellbeing and connection through local action.*

Your mission statement is more than a sentence on your website. It becomes the backbone of your branding and your funding applications. It is the phrase that will anchor you when everything gets busy, the reminder of why you started in the first place.

A Community Interest Company is one of the most flexible and empowering structures available in the UK. It allows you to earn an income while delivering genuine social benefit.

You can access grants that ordinary businesses cannot, and you can trade in ways that charities often cannot.

It is a business with a conscience, a model that gives you the freedom to create something that belongs both to you and to the community you serve.

The best part is that it grows with you. A CIC does not fix you to one role or one idea. It can shift and expand as your ambitions change. You might start with a single project and find it sparks five more. You might launch a local initiative and end up influencing national policy. The structure can hold it all.

Let me tell you about Charlotte. She is a great example of a CIC that started with one idea and then pivoted beyond her wildest dreams. Charlotte wanted to run free self-defence classes for women and girls to help them gain confidence and stay safe. It was an amazing project that quickly got funded by the National Lottery Community Fund and Sport England. But she didn't stop there.

We sat down and explored other options for funding. I encouraged her to think about the Arts Council and the Heritage Lottery. Quite a stretch for someone in the fitness industry and not arts or heritage. But Charlotte was willing to think bigger. We designed two great projects: firstly, a Photography Arts Council project that would photograph women in sport for an exhibition and book, hiring photographers and recruiting sports women. This became a powerful project awarded funding of £30k. Next, we drafted a Heritage Lottery project to research and exhibit the story of women in rugby. Not only this, but she was also awarded UnLtd funding to develop merchandise to sell in her CIC. In just a year, Charlotte now has £67k in grants and some incredible projects for her portfolio that will have a lasting impact, which all came about because she pivoted from that original idea.

Your CIC begins long before the paperwork. It starts the moment you decide your idea deserves a home. Once you understand the structure, everything else begins to make sense. You will see how to register, how to fund and how to grow it into something lasting.

So as you turn the page, keep this in mind. A Community Interest Company is not just a form or a registration number. It is the bridge between your story and the change you want to create. This is where your impact starts to take shape.

Reflection:

- What feels most exciting about creating a structure for your idea – and what still feels intimidating?
- Are you more drawn to the community side of a CIC or to its business potential? Why do you think that is?
- When you picture your community, who are they, and what do they need most right now?
- What difference do you most want your work to make in their lives?
- How could structure help you create that change without burning out or giving too much away for free?

Exercise:

Take a few minutes to sketch the foundations of your future CIC:

1. **Define your community.** Write one sentence that describes who you serve — keep it broad enough to allow growth. Then write one more sentence about how their lives will improve through your work.
2. **List your main activities.** What are the practical ways you will create change? For example, training, workshops, events, mentoring, campaigns or creative projects. Keep your list open and flexible.
3. **Write your first draft mission statement.** Start with "Our mission is to..." and complete the sentence. Don't overthink it. It is a starting point, not a final version.
4. **Check for balance.** Is your CIC idea sustainable? Could you blend grants with trading income, or offer paid services alongside funded work?
5. **Make a note of next steps.** Whether that's researching funders, booking a call with an accountant, or setting aside time to write your CIC36 form, jot down one simple action you can take this week.

When you look back at this exercise later, you will see that these early notes were your first building blocks - the start of turning an idea into something real.

3

My Story: A CIC Journey

By now, you've seen what's possible. You understand what a Community Interest Company is and how it works. But before we move on to building your own, I want to show you something more personal.

While it's one thing to understand the structure, it's another to see how it can completely change a life.

The story I'm about to share isn't just about me. It is about what can happen when you decide to do something different, even when you're scared, unsure or have no idea where to begin. It is proof that a CIC can transform not only your work but your confidence, your freedom and the way you see yourself.

When I look back at where I started, I can hardly believe how far I've come. The transformation still catches me off guard. I owe most of the opportunities that have shaped my life to Community Interest Companies, and I'm endlessly grateful for them.

Back in 2012, I was a probation officer living in a one-bedroom flat in Cornwall. I had done what I was told would lead to a good life. I was the first in my family to go to university, coming from a working-class background where my dad had been a miner. My mum was a single parent by the time I was six. She worked hard, gave me everything she could, and believed with all her heart that education was the key to a better life. Education was hard for me as the school system did not realise I had dyslexia. But I scraped by.

For my mum's generation, university was the answer, and she hadn't had the opportunity to go. If you didn't want a life of struggle, you studied your way out and got a 'good job'. I don't resent that advice; my university years were brilliant. But when I graduated, I had no real understanding of the working world.

I did a master's degree, still unsure what I wanted to do, and I eventually trained to be a probation officer. It was my mum who found the advert for the training scheme. "This will be good for you. They pay you to train," she said. She was right. I wanted to work with people. My original plan had been to become a youth and community worker, but this seemed close enough and, crucially, it was paid.

The job was solid. In seven interesting years, I learned a lot. It gave me stability, a small mortgage and a predictable life. But after a while, I couldn't help wondering, *is this it?* The only promotion available was to become a manager. I didn't even particularly like my managers, let alone want to be one of them. That didn't feel like a dream to chase.

So I started chasing something else.

The Spark That Changed Everything

Outside of work, I'd always had creative hobbies. I took photography classes in the evenings, and soon I was dreaming of starting a studio. At the same time, I ran a music project with offenders in prison called Rap Therapy. It combined creativity with rehabilitation, and somehow it worked. We even won an award for innovation.

That project showed me something I hadn't quite realised before: I had ideas that worked with hard-to-reach young people, and I wanted to do more of it.

One of my colleagues said, "Kelly, this would make a great CIC."

I had no idea what that meant. But when he explained that I could get grant funding and run this kind of project independently, something in me lit up. I started to imagine a future in which my love for creativity and my passion for community work could coexist.

At first, I thought a CIC might just supplement my income from my photography business. I knew making a living as a photographer would be tough; weddings and family shoots weren't going to make me rich. But the thought of running community projects as part of my work was exciting.

It turned out to be more than exciting. It was life-changing.

Starting a CIC gave me a sense of control I'd never had before. It was the perfect balance. I could build a business, gain funding and create impact all at once. Starting any business is hard, but starting one that can access grants is a complete game-changer.

From Probation Officer to Purpose-Led Entrepreneur

The first grants I received were large, lump-sum payments. That made life easier straight away. For the first time, I could pay debts, save a deposit and plan ahead. My income suddenly looked healthy to mortgage lenders, and soon I was able to buy a three-bedroom new-build house on my own.

I remember that morning vividly, standing in the middle of my brand-new kitchen, realising that everything I'd worked for had led here. It wasn't a mansion. It wasn't luxury. But it was mine. And it felt like winning the lottery.

For someone from my background - single mum, working class, no safety net - that was massive. It proved that purpose-led work could be financially stable too.

From there, things snowballed. My photography business and my CIC complemented each other perfectly. The studio gave me the space, equipment and professional base I needed. The CIC brought in the grant funding and the projects. Each supported the other.

I earned more than I ever had as a probation officer. I travelled more too. I could take time off when I needed it, work on creative projects, and feel proud of the difference I was making. I didn't really need to grow a big CIC, because at that time the cost of living was much lower, so I was working very successfully from my house, travelling, running great projects and getting paid for it. It was the heyday of CICs, for sure. So, I was happy just running a few great projects on my own.

Projects That Shaped My Life

Over the years, my CIC ran countless projects: youth arts, heritage and history, school engagement, creative rehabilitation, community media. One week I'd be teaching photography in a youth centre, the next I'd be helping ex-offenders write a course for prisons.

It suited me perfectly. I have always had a restless mind; I get bored quickly, and a CIC gave me the freedom to keep moving, to keep learning. It became a vehicle for my creativity. I suspect I have ADHD, though I've never sought a diagnosis. I don't need one. I have learned to work with the way my mind moves: fast, curious, constantly on to the next idea. A CIC allows that. You can take one project, build it, deliver it, and then start something new. It keeps life interesting.

But it wasn't just good for me. The impact on the community was real. I watched young people find confidence, move into work and step away from crime. I received constant messages of thanks from professionals, parents and participants. The work mattered, and it showed.

My projects took me far beyond Cornwall, photographing street art from New York City to Australia. The most special project was in The Gambia, where I worked with a children's education charity to help build schools and create media for their cause. Those experiences deepened everything. Seeing global inequality up close changed how I thought about my own community, my privilege and my purpose.

Ten years on, my portfolio was enormous. My CV wouldn't fit on the page. I had worked with national funders, delivered dozens of projects, and built something I could barely have imagined when I was sitting in that one-bedroom flat.

It wasn't all easy, though. The paperwork, evaluation and rejected applications were all stressful. I made mistakes and tripped up, mainly because I was on my own and didn't know how it was supposed to work. It was not as simple as getting an accountant – they also don't always know how CICs work. I think, as they are relatively new and there are no real guidelines, even the grant funders contradict themselves about the 'rules'. There was clearly a need to help and give guidance to CICs.

This led me to the next chapter of my story.

CIC Tribe

Ten years of grant funding led me to a newfound career that unintentionally exploded into my life. I kept being asked how to set up a CIC and to write people's grants. I poured everything I know into a course and a YouTube Channel. Funny to think a course I filmed in my front room one day has changed the lives of thousands of people. This was totally unintended.

I put one video on YouTube and the course for sale and left it. When I went back, I was blown away to see I had six hundred views and fifty sales! I had filled a gap in knowledge that was in demand. So, I took it more seriously and started filling out my YouTube Channel with my CIC tips and knowledge. I expanded into packages for grant writing and consultant calls. I even started a membership to help CICs in a supportive community. The success stories rolled in, and it gained incredible attention. CIC Tribe was born.

Becoming a grant writer for others was life-changing. The skills I learned not only helped me with my own grants, but meant I could be paid to write grants for other people and their CICs. This took over, and soon I had too much demand, so I started hiring my most successful students as experts and grant writers. It was no longer just me anymore. I had launched a national CIC movement and community.

Our success statistics are insane. Because we are real people with real CICs, we have more success in guiding others. I very much think that our systems and strategies are successful because we have experienced CIC owners' struggles ourselves, and we share solutions that create success.

Your Story and Why It Matters

Every CIC begins with a story. Sometimes it is a story of frustration, sometimes of heartbreak, and sometimes simply of noticing a gap that no one else has filled. Our stories are what drive us to act.

When I first started my own CIC, I didn't have a clear blueprint. I had experience, a reason, and a feeling that something needed to change. It is often like that. The moment you stop waiting for permission and decide to do something with what you know, that is when the work begins.

People often ask how much of their personal story they should share. The answer depends on the situation. Your story matters deeply, but you do not always need to tell it in full detail. On a grant application, the focus should be on your community, not you as an individual. A Community Interest Company is a structure that represents a shared cause. When you write your forms, write as the CIC, not as the founder.

Save your personal story for the places where it truly connects with people. Use it in your social media, on your website and in your conversations. People relate to honesty. They are drawn to lived experience. Your story is what will bring others to your community, but funders need evidence, planning and impact. They are two sides of the same coin.

If you decide to share your story publicly, share it with purpose. You do not need to expose every detail of your life to prove your commitment. Focus on the lessons and the solutions your experience has taught you. If you have lived through something difficult, speak about how it shaped your understanding and what positive change came from it. Vulnerability without direction can feel heavy. Vulnerability with intent builds trust.

Many of the most successful CICs are built from lived experience. People who have seen a problem up close tend to design solutions that work. I see it constantly within the CIC Tribe community. Someone who has faced healthcare inequality creates a support network for others like them. A parent who has struggled to find accessible activities for their child builds a project that fills that gap. Lived experience is not a limitation. It is expertise.

The key is to translate that experience into professional language that funders and partners can understand. When you describe your work, use phrases like 'community-led' or 'founded by people with lived experience of...' rather than writing from a deeply personal point of view. It shows empathy and credibility without oversharing.

If your story feels painful, that is okay. You do not need to rush to make sense of it. The process of creating something positive out of something difficult can be deeply healing. You might find that the more you focus on helping others, the more your own confidence and clarity grow.

Remember, this work is not about perfection. You do not need to have every answer before you start. You only need the willingness to act. The rest you learn along the way.

So, use your story wisely. Let it guide you without defining you. Let it inspire others, but do not let it drain you. A CIC is a bridge between who you are and what you can offer the world. Your story is simply the foundation.

Lessons From the Harder Days

In CIC Tribe, we make solutions out of the mistakes and hardships experienced by CICs – my own and others'. The mistakes and challenges in my CIC early days taught me as much as the successes I had.

One of the hardest early lessons came from a fallout with a childhood friend who was a director in my first CIC. We didn't see eye to eye, and it damaged both the business and the friendship. It taught me something I now tell everyone I mentor: be very careful who you go into partnership with. Friendship doesn't automatically translate to shared vision or shared responsibility. I turn this into a lesson for my new CICs, and I make sure they choose their partners carefully and have a director's contract.

I also learned the hard way that you can't always hire people just because you want to help them. Early on, I brought in people who were struggling financially, hoping to give them experience and income. Sometimes it worked beautifully.

Other times, they couldn't deliver or be relied on. I had overestimated their commitment or readiness. It taught me to separate compassion from recruitment. You can still help people, but you need boundaries if you want your CIC to thrive. I see CICs trying to hire their family members and children to help them earn. I tell them this is a bad idea. I have helped many people avoid big mistakes by using cautionary tales from my own or other CICs.

Another challenge was paperwork. I am dyslexic, and admin has never been my strong point. I hated evaluation forms and financial reports. There were times I didn't keep the best records, and times I was fined by Companies House simply because I didn't know what needed submitting. It is easy to trip up when you're new and learning as you go. CICs are different from regular companies, and more often than not I see CICs getting the wrong advice from accountants who don't know what's best for a CIC either. How are CIC owners supposed to get it right if they don't know what they don't know? So now I give video guides and templates.

Those experiences became part of the reason I built CIC Tribe the way I did, with systems, checklists and support to stop others from making the same mistakes, and bringing in real-world CIC owners as experts so the CIC Tribe members get the benefit of their experience. I wanted to create a smoother path for the next wave of founders so they could spend more time making impact and less time fighting bureaucracy.

Where It's All Led

Now, years later, I still run a thriving local art hub CIC (@ oberi_art) alongside my main business. I share it with my husband and a friend, and we focus on community arts. I do this just one morning a week, but I love it. I have learned alternatives to grant funding for this CIC, which is great, as it means less work and regulation. It keeps me grounded. It reminds me why I started all this in the first place.

Even if I were a billionaire, I'd still have a CIC. To me, it's the most fulfilling kind of hobby, one that benefits everyone involved.

Running a CIC gives you the ability to channel funding directly into causes you care about, to create opportunities for others, and to build a legacy that goes beyond profit. If I want to give back, I don't need to go through complicated charitable structures or tax loopholes. I can just run a project, employ local people and see the impact unfold.

That is what I love most. The simplicity. The accessibility. The fact that anyone, from any background, can take their skills, their story, and their heart for the community and turn them into something powerful.

My CIC work still connects me to local artists, young people and community spaces. It gives students work experience they can't get elsewhere, helps creative professionals find their footing, and keeps the arts alive in small towns that need it most.

When I look at my life now, I'm humbled. CICs have given me freedom, purpose and community. They have changed my finances, my confidence, my outlook and the lives of thousands of others along the way.

The knock-on effects are astronomical, and I'll never stop being amazed by them.

Looking Ahead

My journey hasn't been perfect, but it's proof of what's possible when passion meets purpose and structure. Community Interest Companies have transformed my life, and now they transform the lives of others through the work I do every day.

If my story proves anything, it's that a CIC isn't just paperwork. It is a catalyst. It starts with one person deciding to act.

In the next chapter, I'll take you through how to build your own CIC, not just one that exists on paper, but one that's sustainable, fulfilling and built to last. You don't need permission to make an impact. You just need the right foundation.

Reflection:

- What moments or experiences in your life have shaped the kind of change you want to make?
- How does your story connect to the people you most want to help?
- When you think about sharing your story, what feels empowering and what feels uncomfortable?
- How can you use your story to inspire trust without oversharing or losing focus on your community?

- What strengths or insights has your lived experience given you that others might not have?

Exercise:

Take time to map your story and turn it into purpose.

1. Write down three key moments that changed how you see the world. These could be personal challenges, moments of success, or situations that opened your eyes to a gap or injustice.
2. For each moment, note what it taught you. What skills, empathy or understanding came from it? How does that insight shape the work you want to do?
3. Draw a simple line from 'experience' to 'impact'. For example:
   Experience: "I struggled to access mental health support."
   Impact: "Now I help others find affordable wellbeing services."
4. Create a short version of your story. Imagine you are introducing yourself at a community event. In two or three sentences, explain what inspired your work and who you help. Keep it honest, simple and positive.
5. Reflect on how it feels to tell it. If it feels heavy, focus more on what you've learned and less on what you've lost. If it feels energising, you've found the right tone.

Your story is not a script to perform. It is a thread that runs through everything you build. When you can speak about where you've come from with clarity and compassion, you'll find that people lean in – not because you've struggled, but because you've turned that struggle into strength.

4
Building the Right Structure

By now, you've seen what a CIC can achieve and how structure can change a life. This is where we get practical, where your vision starts taking shape on paper.

Setting up a Community Interest Company can feel complicated at first. The jargon, the forms, the questions about what to include and who to involve: it can all seem like a foreign language. Many people walk into it blind, unsure what lies ahead. This chapter will ease you through that process and help you build the kind of structure that sets your CIC up for success.

When you understand the foundations properly, everything else becomes easier. Your projects run more smoothly, funders trust you more quickly, and you start your journey from a place of confidence rather than confusion.

The Legal Foundations

A Community Interest Company should be set up as a company limited by guarantee. This means there are no shares or dividends. Any profit your organisation makes is reinvested directly back into your mission.

You will also need an 'asset lock'. This ensures that all assets and funds within the CIC are used for the benefit of the community you serve. If the CIC ever closes, what remains must be passed to another community organisation or charity, not to individuals.

These legal features protect your integrity and reassure funders that their money is being used properly. They are what make the CIC structure such a trusted model for social impact. You can still trade and sell services just as a limited company would, but your mission is always to serve your community, the one you will define in your governing documents and on your CIC36 form.

I remember the first time I saw the term 'asset lock'. It sounded intimidating, like something from a corporate handbook. But once I understood it, I realised it was actually my shield, the safeguard that would protect the integrity of my mission and stop anyone from twisting my purpose for profit. Once that clicked, the legal language stopped feeling cold and started to make sense.

Defining Your Community and Governing Documents

The registration process will ask you to describe who your community is. This matters more than most people realise. Write clearly and honestly about who will benefit from your work, but avoid boxing yourself in. If you make it too narrow, you might have to amend your documents later when your projects evolve.

A good example might look like this:

"We support young people aged 16–25 who are not in education, employment or training through creative workshops and mentoring programmes."

That kind of sentence is specific enough to show purpose but broad enough to grow.

Once you have finalised your community description and activities, these details will appear in your governing documents (your Articles of Association and your CIC36 form), both of which will be submitted to Companies House when you register. At that point, your CIC officially exists.

That small moment, clicking 'submit', is when an idea becomes a legal entity. For many people, it is one of the most empowering steps they ever take.

Choosing Your Directors

You will need at least three directors to form your CIC. They must be unrelated, which means they cannot share your surname, live at your address or be immediate family members.

Be careful when choosing who to invite onto your board. This is where many new founders make mistakes. The wrong directors can create tension and misunderstandings, and might even put your CIC at risk. Choosing directors can be surprisingly personal. You might be tempted to ask friends or family because you trust them, but business and friendship often mix poorly. It is far better to build a board of people who believe in your mission and respect your leadership.

Directors are legally responsible for the company, but their roles are voluntary. They are not paid for simply being directors. It is vital you set those expectations clearly from the start. If someone expects to be paid for their involvement, they should instead be hired as a freelancer on specific projects, not appointed as a director. As the founding director, you can be paid for the delivery of work, for example, facilitating groups, running workshops or managing projects, but not for holding the directorship itself. This distinction keeps your CIC compliant and protects its funding eligibility.

I like to use the terms of founding director and supporting director. These are not official terms, but they help you and your directors understand your roles. Officially, you all have to have equal voting rights, but in reality and in practice, this CIC is your baby. You just want a couple of people on the board to support you so you can 'do your thing'. Tip: choose people who don't know each other so won't vote you down; choose people who are unlikely to try to take the CIC from you or expect something in future. Aim for supportive people who are not going to get too involved.

Building the Right Structure and Team

When you first decide to set up a CIC, one of the earliest challenges is finding the right people to stand beside you. Directors are part of the legal requirement, but they are also part of your safety net. Choose them with care.

The best place to start is with people who genuinely want to help and who understand your values. They do not need to be experts or have experience in your field. What matters most is reliability, integrity and a willingness to say yes to the journey. Before you ask anyone to become a director, have a quiet think about what that really means. Being a director does not take up huge amounts of time, but it is still a responsibility. They need to be comfortable signing documents, attending occasional meetings, and being associated with the work your CIC delivers. They should understand what the organisation does and what is expected of them.

There are practical checks to make as well. Directors cannot be bankrupt or under certain financial restrictions, such as insolvency or specific voluntary arrangements, because these can cause issues with banking. Ask gently but directly about this. Early transparency is always better than awkward surprises later. It is also worth checking whether they are already serving as a director on another CIC or charity board. If someone sits on several, funders might question how active or committed they can be. One or two roles are fine. Any more can become a red flag.

Then there is the personal side. You want directors who will not overstep. Some people mean well but end up trying to steer the ship. Remember that as the founder, you are the driving force. Your directors are there to support and oversee, not to take control. Avoid bringing in people who have a close personal connection with each other. If two directors already have a strong bond, they could potentially outvote you if decisions ever became difficult. It sounds dramatic, but it happens. Choose independence over convenience.

A simple written agreement at the start makes everything easier. Even though every director has equal voting rights in law, a clear understanding of roles and expectations can prevent misunderstandings. Put it in a short contract that everyone signs. You might include things like agreeing to step down if values no longer align with the CIC, understanding that the position is unpaid, reviewing director roles each year, and seeking board approval before using your position for personal gain. A clear, signed document saves stress later.

Add a short code of conduct, too. It sets a professional tone without being heavy-handed. If there is ever a serious issue, the other directors can vote to remove someone who breaches that code. Most boards never need to use it, but knowing the system is there gives everyone peace of mind.

Directors can change in the future. People move, change jobs or need a break. As long as they agree to resign and the change is recorded properly with Companies House, it is straightforward. What matters most is that your board feels safe and balanced. These are the people who will help you make big decisions, approve your accounts and act as guardians of your mission. They do not need to be loud or charismatic. They just need to care.

Boundaries matter. Choose directors who share your passion and integrity, but who also understand that their role is about guidance and accountability, not personal gain. When you get this part right, it gives your CIC a sense of structure and stability that you will feel in every project you run. It allows you to lead confidently, knowing that there are people in your corner who understand what you are trying to build and will help you protect it.

Getting Your Basics in Place

Once your CIC is registered and your directors are confirmed, it is time to get the basics sorted. You will be working closely with communities, so make sure your essential policies are in place: safeguarding, data protection, equality and diversity, health and safety and insurance.

These policies are more than paperwork. They prove to funders that you are serious, responsible and ready to deliver projects safely.

Start small. Keep your first year simple and focused. Run a few manageable projects that allow you to learn how to apply for grants, deliver activities and record outcomes. It is far better to run three small, well-executed projects than one overly ambitious one that leaves you exhausted and overwhelmed.

Starting small builds trust, with yourself as much as with funders. Every project you complete proves you can deliver, and that confidence becomes your best marketing.

In your first year, think about projects like local workshops, community events or support groups. These are achievable and give you the experience you need to manage budgets, report outcomes and build credibility with funders. Larger, more complex work, such as contracts with the NHS, projects in prisons, or premises development, can come later. Year two and beyond will bring bigger opportunities once you have evidence of impact.

Many of the CICs I work with secure funding in their very first year, sometimes well over £100,000 combined from different funders. The key is to start with focus, clarity and commitment. Once you have proved that your projects deliver results, more funding will follow naturally.

Running Day-to-Day Operations

As a CIC founder, you will wear many hats. You will be a manager, administrator, fundraiser, marketer and sometimes cleaner all in one. It is demanding but deeply rewarding. You will handle paperwork, funding applications and project management while also delivering workshops, updating social media and maintaining your accounts.

In the beginning, I ran sessions during the day and wrote funding bids at midnight. It was messy, exhausting and brilliant all at once. The trick is not perfection; it is persistence.

The best advice I can give is this: do not try to do it all alone. Build a small network of volunteers or collaborators to help you. This might include people from your community who want to contribute their skills, students seeking experience or professionals who believe in your cause.

Whenever possible, use freelancers for project delivery rather than employing full-time staff in the early years. Most grant-funded work is time-limited. Hiring freelancers gives you flexibility, keeps costs manageable, and avoids the added responsibilities of PAYE and national insurance. And remember, it is perfectly fine to pay yourself as a freelancer within your own CIC for the delivery work you do. That is both lawful and expected.

Complementary Business Structures

Alongside your CIC, you may also choose to operate as a sole trader or limited company. This can be a clever way to balance your personal business interests with your social impact work.

For example, you might run a CIC that delivers community workshops while also having a limited company through which you sell professional training or creative products. Keeping these separate allows you to protect your personal intellectual property.

If you develop a course, a book or any original material for your CIC, and you create it within the CIC itself, then the CIC legally owns it. That means you cannot take it back later or use it independently. If you produce it through your own business, you can then license it to your CIC, ensuring both you and the organisation benefit fairly.

This kind of structure is not about greed. It is about sustainability and protecting your work. You are both a community leader and a social entrepreneur, and it is entirely right to build something that serves both the public and your future. It also gives you creative freedom. You can develop ideas without feeling tied to one structure, which keeps both you and your CIC flexible and fresh.

Some CIC owners will just want to have a CIC and think that is easier, and many accountants will encourage this. But it's not practical. Grant funders will want you to pay yourself as a freelancer, not as an employee. This is because a grant project is temporary. So, you will have to set up as self-employed or a limited company. To be in line with HMRC rules, that business will need to have more than the CIC as income. You will need to earn something else in your limited/self-employed business. Also, *you* will want to, as this is your social enterprise *and* your opportunity to grow a profit-making business.

I advise you to have a simple social enterprise, so you don't burn out. Running a CIC and an limited/self-employed business can be overwhelming. So, keep it simple. I have a whole other strategy for a social enterprise called the Purpose Plan, but that will be in my second book! For now, just bear in mind that you will need to work on this sister business after you set up your CIC and start earning through grants.

Paying Yourself Fairly

There is no shame in paying yourself appropriately for the work you do. Too many social entrepreneurs fall into the trap of thinking they must live on scraps to prove their integrity. That mindset only leads to burnout and resentment.

Research shows that founders who underpay themselves are far more likely to close their organisations within two years. You cannot pour from an empty cup. You are doing work that benefits society, often delivering projects and support for a fraction of what the government would pay for the same outcomes. You are value for money. You are skilled, passionate and dedicated.

It is important to structure your CIC in a way that keeps you sustainable. Paying yourself for your time, budgeting fairly for project delivery and building financial security are not selfish acts; they allow your organisation to last. Sustainability is not just about funding and strategy. It is about you. If you burn out, your CIC burns out with you. Look after yourself as seriously as you look after your mission.

Building for the Long Term

As your CIC grows, your structure will evolve. You may take on larger grants, employ staff or even expand into new regions. But the same principles apply at every stage: clear governance, transparent finances and a strong sense of purpose.

Every time I see a founder finally register their CIC, I think of what it represents. Not paperwork... Possibility. A chance to rewrite what work, community and success can look like.

Remember that impact takes time. Every project, every report, every connection you build adds to your reputation and your reach. What starts as a small, local effort can grow into something extraordinary.

The key is structure, not as red tape, but as a framework for freedom. When you build your CIC on the right foundations, you give yourself the stability to dream bigger.

In Summary

This chapter was about the practical side of creating your CIC, the parts that might seem dry on paper but are actually what make everything else possible. Get your structure right, choose your directors wisely, protect your work and value your own contribution. Do that, and you will create something that can grow, thrive and change lives, including your own.

Reflect:

- What do you want out of your CIC?
- How much time do you want to give?
- Who do you want as directors?

Exercise:

Create a short list of five adjectives that describe your dream CIC life. Then write one sentence that captures your tone, such as, "I want to be a _____ leader in my community." Use this as the anchor for how you design your projects.

5

Branding and Social Media

You have done the hard bit. You have brought your CIC to life. You have gone from idea to registration, from dream to structure. But now comes the part that decides whether people find you, trust you and fund you.

Visibility is power.

Branding and social media are not decoration. They are how people understand who you are, what you stand for and whether they can believe in your work. They are also how funders, partners and your community decide if they can trust you with their time, money or participation.

Every time you apply for a grant, someone checks your social media. Funders look at it when you apply and again when your project ends. They want to see proof of activity, community engagement and the difference their funding made.

The same goes for partners and local authorities. Even the people you serve – parents, carers, young people, perhaps – will check your pages before getting involved. They want to know your work is credible, active and safe. That is why your presence matters.

Why Branding Matters

Think of branding as your organisation's identity. It is not you as a person, remember. If your CIC's mission is the heartbeat, your branding is the face. It is what people recognise, remember and talk about when you are not in the room.

I have seen founders change everything simply by getting this part right. Jasmin (Countryside Connect CIC) from my CIC Tribe rebranded her community farm to a CIC, redesigned her logo, and began sharing her projects consistently on social media. She made fun TikTok videos about life on the farm, running her home-schooling project. Her community grew, and within months she attracted over £64k in grants in year one. She will also easily be able to prove her activities happened, as there is a good social media footprint for the duration of the projects.

Branding does not need to be expensive or fancy. It just needs to be clear and consistent. You want people to look at your posts, your website, your flyers, and instantly know it is you.

Your branding begins with clarity: who you are, what you do, and how you want people to feel when they encounter your work.

Start with your logo and colour palette. Choose colours that fit your tone and audience. Warm tones feel welcoming, bold ones feel energetic, and neutral tones feel professional. Once you have chosen, use them everywhere: your flyers, your website, your social media headers. Consistency builds recognition, and recognition builds trust.

A brilliant free tool for this is Canva. It is an easy design platform where you can make everything from social media graphics to banners. CICs can even apply for a free Canva Pro account through their not-for-profit scheme.

Set up your brand kit in Canva with your colours, fonts and logo. That way, every piece of content looks cohesive and professional without much effort.

Branding, Visibility and Building Trust

When most people think about running a business, they imagine constant posting on social media, endless promotion and the pressure to sell. A Community Interest Company is different. Your purpose is to serve, and that means your presence should reflect trust, connection and authenticity.

You do not need to be on every platform or constantly in front of the camera. The best approach to social media for a CIC is steady, simple and real. Share photographs of your activities, stories from your community and updates about your projects. Let people see the work happening behind the scenes. You do not need a marketing strategy that looks corporate or forced. A consistent flow of small, honest updates will say far more about who you are.

Think of your online presence as an open window into your world. People are naturally curious. They want to see what their grant funding supports, how participants benefit and what difference you make. A single photo of a smiling group at a workshop or a quick post celebrating new funding can go further than a dozen perfectly designed graphics.

If the thought of social media makes you anxious, remember that you do not need to do everything yourself. You can invite volunteers, team members or participants to help share updates. The voice of your community is often far more powerful than your own.

Sometimes people worry about what to do if things turn negative online. The truth is, it rarely happens. Most people understand that a CIC exists for good reason and will respect the effort behind your work. On the rare occasion you face criticism, treat it like any other form of damage control. Stay calm, remove anything abusive, and respond only when a genuine question deserves an answer. Never get pulled into public arguments.

Occasionally, jealousy can appear. It might come from others in your sector or even within your local area. Perhaps someone is frustrated by your success or by the fact that you have received funding. It happens. The best protection is transparency. If your accounts are clear, your paperwork is up to date and your delivery is solid, no complaint can truly harm you. You are answerable to your funders, not to gossip.

I have seen rare cases in which jealousy has gone as far as false allegations and even reports to funders. The key lesson from those experiences is simple: be meticulous. Have your safeguarding policies signed and dated, keep digital copies of your paperwork and document everything. If an audit ever happens, you will have nothing to fear.

What keeps your reputation strong is not perfection, it is integrity. If you make a mistake, acknowledge it and fix it. If you have success, celebrate it openly and thank the people who made it possible. People remember honesty.

Branding, at its heart, is about consistency. Use the same name, logo and tone of voice wherever you appear. Keep it warm, human and aligned with your cause. If your work supports families, your tone should feel welcoming. If it focuses on youth, keep it energetic and inclusive. Your branding should help people recognise you instantly as the organisation they can trust.

Above all, never feel that you must appear larger than you are. Authenticity beats scale every time. Show the real people behind the project. That is what builds credibility.

When you think of social media as storytelling rather than marketing, everything changes. It stops feeling like work and starts feeling like connection. Each post becomes a small thank you to your community and a reminder of why you do what you do.

Creating an Online Presence

Once your branding feels right, it is time to make sure people can see you.

Start with Facebook and Instagram. These are the two main platforms funders, partners and the public will check. If your CIC is brand new, do not worry about follower numbers. What matters is that your page looks active and authentic.

Share updates from your projects. Post photos of your events and tag the people and organisations involved. Most funders ask that you publicly thank them, and social media is an easy way to do that.

During your projects, post regularly. Give short updates, quotes from participants and snippets of what is happening. When the project finishes, funders will go back and look at your page. If they can see the journey unfold, your impact speaks for itself.

Social media also gives you visibility within your community. People who might never find your website will see your posts, recognise your name and begin to follow what you do. That is free marketing and storytelling rolled into one.

Invest in Meta Ads for Facebook and Instagram. This will grow your community online and lead them to your signups on your website for events or free digital downloads which give value. This is really helpful as growing an email list is vital for all businesses, even CICs. This is often overlooked by CICs, as people think about grant funding but not all the usual business sales income streams that come from having a good online audience and email list.

None of this needs to take up all your time. Nor do you need funding to hire a professional. Just start simple: create in batches and post using scheduling. I spend a couple of hours a month scheduling posts to drop a couple per week over the course of a month. Easy tip: take eight images and videos at a workshop and schedule them to post twice a week for a month. Use a call to action for people to sign up to a mailing list, RSVP to an event or download a free PDF with valuable info.

Building Connection and Community

If you want deeper engagement, create a Facebook group alongside your main page. A group lets people belong to something, to feel part of your mission. It is particularly effective if you work with adults, families or local residents.

A group can become a hub for conversation, peer support and feedback. You can share opportunities, promote events and ask for volunteers. It is a simple way to nurture your community without needing constant one-to-one communication.

Here is a great example. One of my CIC students, Jo, has a menopause Facebook group with over six thousand members. This is great for her level of impact because she can help six thousand women from all over the country. It also makes it easy to deliver. She was able to get enough funding from the National Lottery Community Fund to keep this group running for two years with some community meet-ups. The Facebook group is the core of her CIC. Having that community means she can sell her retreats, books and paid membership. But for free, they still get tons of value, support, peer-to-peer help and advice, which also helps take the time and pressure off Jo as the community starts to help each other.

This is a great example of an online community that creates a sustainable CIC with a massive impact in the long term.

WhatsApp can work just as well for smaller, more focused groups. It is informal, personal and easy to manage. You can use it for project participants or community members who need a quick way to stay connected.

Groups and chats are more than tools. They are living proof of community impact. Funders love seeing evidence of networks that exist because of your work.

Expanding With Video, TikTok and YouTube

Once you have your basics running, consider adding video platforms. TikTok and YouTube are powerful for raising awareness and showcasing your projects.

TikTok is great for visibility. Short clips can reach thousands of people quickly, spreading your message far beyond your local area. You can show behind-the-scenes moments, snippets from events, or quick facts about your cause. Funders often love to see creative outreach like this; it demonstrates innovation and public engagement.

YouTube, on the other hand, is your long-term storytelling tool. It is your legacy content: that means it stays up and is viewed long term; it is not lost after just a few minutes. It allows you to build a permanent library of videos that continue to share your impact long after a project ends.

You might record workshops, film short interviews with participants, or share reflective videos about what your team has learned. Keep them simple and real. You do not need professional equipment, just honesty and a steady camera.

When applying for grants, include links to your videos. Let funders see and hear the people whose lives you are changing. They will feel the emotion that words on a page cannot deliver. This is my top tip for getting your applications awarded the first time: I always get my students to put a YouTube link to a short video of their taster session and participants' feedback.

As your CIC grows, you will use the YouTube channel in different projects, not just for evidence of your project but as part of your project itself. I have included a YouTube video presentation on a Heritage project as one of the outcomes. This presents the history of projects, research and findings. The Heritage Lottery loves this as it can be accessed by many people in the long term. Likewise, I have included YouTube music videos and performances as outcomes in Arts Council projects. Again, it gives accessible long-term audiences.

So instead of viewing social media as just a necessary admin task for building a presence, use it in your grant projects for impact and long-term engagement.

Your Website and Email List

Social media is brilliant, but you also need a central home, a website where everything connects. Many CIC owners get this wrong.

The most common mistake is to pay someone to set up a website using a code-based website builder like WordPress. This is both a waste of money and extremely bad for the CIC's business. This makes a static website the CIC owner cannot do anything with and needs to pay to update. The site sits there, doing nothing. This is a terrible idea, because you need more than a website: you need a booking system, online sales, and an email list to gather and nurture with regular emails. You need all of this on your website, and Wix is by far the best platform for this. I have made a CIC template website with Wix for my CIC Tribe members to download and use. It is cheap and easy to build and maintain yourself. Even if you pay someone to do the basics, you will still be able to use its functions like email and sales.

In terms of layout, your website does not have to be complicated. A few clear pages are enough. Here is a basic list for your menu:

- Home page - mission statement
- About page - details about your CIC and directors
- Project pages - list your projects (great for grant funders to check; do a page on each)
- Shop - Sell merchandise and digital assets like eBooks
- Price plans - online course and/or memberships
- Events - RSVP to free and paid events
- Lead generator page - This could be a landing page to sign up for a free ebook or PDF which gives value. This enables you to gather and grow an email list.
- Fundraising page - Campaigns to raise funds and donation links to JustGiving or Crowdfunder.

Email lists are gold for any CIC. They give you direct communication with your supporters, partners and participants. You do not have to rely on algorithms or timing; you can reach your audience whenever you have something important to share.

Offer something small but valuable in exchange for signing up: a guide, a resource list or an activity sheet related to your work. It does not need to be fancy, just something genuinely helpful.

Make sure your website matches your branding. Every colour, every word and every image should feel part of the same story.

Link with your socials to create a funnel. For example, post on Instagram to promote your free eBook ⊠ link to website landing page to capture email ⊠ they get a download, and you get an email address. Boosting the post using paid ads will do wonders to grow your community.

Showing Up as the Founder

Your CIC's brand and your personal brand are connected, but you need to remember that you are a community. Be careful not to make your CIC platforms all about you. You are the main face and voice of your organisation, but this needs to be combined with the faces and voices of your community as well. People will associate your energy, values and personality with your CIC's mission. It is fine for you to be the main content maker, especially if your content is delivering information and value.

This does not mean turning yourself into the brand. It means being visible as a real, trustworthy human. Share the occasional behind-the-scenes moment, a day preparing for an event, an honest reflection, a proud success. People invest in people, not logos.

Keep your CIC social media professional but warm. Make sure it is full of community and visible impact. If you can, invest in a few professional photos or short video clips. If money is tight, reach out to local colleges or universities. Photography or media students often need projects to build their portfolios and will work with you for free or at a small cost.

You do not need to look polished, just real. Confident. Passionate.

Feeling Overwhelmed?

If this all feels like a lot, take a breath. You do not need to do everything at once.

Start with the basics: get your logo, start your Facebook and Instagram page, and make a few posts. Once that feels steady, move on to your website or email list. Gradual, consistent progress always beats perfection.

Social media and branding are skills like any other. You will learn what works for you as you go. The important thing is to start showing up.

In Summary

Your CIC can have the best mission in the world, but if no one can see it online, funders will mistrust you.

Branding and social media are not vanity projects. They are your bridge to opportunity, how you attract funders, how you reach communities and how you prove your impact.

Visibility builds credibility. Credibility builds partnerships. Partnerships build sustainability.

And that is where we are heading next. In the next chapter, we will explore how to turn all this visibility into opportunity, contracts, collaborations and long-term partnerships that will help your CIC grow.

Reflection:

- How do you feel about social media?
- What types of content do you think you will focus on?
- What could you offer as a freebie download that your community would want?

Exercise:

List three small branding goals for the next six months. For each, write one practical first step, such as 'create my freebie' or 'draft a simple social media plan'. Progress begins with clarity, not perfection.

6
Financial Confidence and Sustainability

You have built something real. You have registered, branded and started showing the world who you are. Now comes the question that every founder quietly worries about: how do I make this work financially?

Money can be the most confusing part of running a CIC. You can ask ten people how to pay yourself or how to stay legitimate, and you will get ten different answers. Accountants get it wrong, funders get it wrong, and well-meaning peers often pass on myths that make things sound harder than they are.

So let us clear it up.

This chapter is about helping you understand how to pay yourself properly, how to manage your money within the rules, and how to build something that lasts. Because without financial clarity, your CIC will not just struggle, it will not survive.

The Emotional Side of Money

Money is an emotional topic, especially for people who lead with heart. You probably did not start your CIC because you love spreadsheets or budgets. You started it because you care. But caring does not pay the rent. And that tension, between purpose and practicality, can leave you torn.

I have been there. I know the guilt of paying myself when others needed help. I have also felt the exhaustion that comes from not doing it. For many people in the social enterprise world, money feels like the one subject that still carries shame. But it should not.

Money is not a measure of greed. It is a measure of energy and exchange. When you are paid fairly for your work, you can keep showing up, keep giving, and keep building impact. When you are not, your passion slowly burns out.

It is time to remove the guilt and replace it with understanding.

The Truth About CIC Finances

There is a lot of confusion about what not-for-profit actually means. It does not mean you cannot make money. It means the organisation itself does not distribute profits for private gain. You can still pay yourself fairly for your time, your skills and your leadership.

Funders expect you to. They do not want you to run yourself into the ground. They want your CIC to be well-managed, sustainable, and led by people who can keep going in the long term.

Unfortunately, some accountants do not understand CICs properly. They treat them like charities or like limited companies, when they are neither. As a result, it is easy to end up feeling confused about what is allowed.

I have been through this myself, and after more than a decade of working with thousands of CIC founders, I have found the balance. It is not complicated once you know how.

Common Financial Myths

Let us break a few common myths I hear all the time.

- **You cannot pay yourself from a grant.**
  You can, as long as it is included in your project budget and approved by the funder. They expect you to be paid for delivery.
- **You have to be a charity to get serious funding.**
  You do not. CICs receive millions in grant funding every year, often more flexibly than charities do. However, it is true that charities can get some grants that CICs cannot access.
- **You must do everything yourself to save money.**
  You do not. Paying for professional help, such as bookkeeping or graphic design, is legitimate spending if it supports your project delivery. You can and should include other freelancers on your project budgets.
- **Taking pay means you are not community-minded.**
  Not true. Being sustainable allows you to serve more people, more consistently, without burning out. You are paid in line with National Standards, and a CIC should have a modern-day slavery

policy. Volunteering is fine, but your CIC has responsibilities to volunteers by law.

Myth-busting is not about defending yourself. It is about owning your right to build something strong and lasting.

Paying Yourself the Right Way

If you feel uneasy about paying yourself, you are not alone. Many founders do. They have been conditioned to believe that purpose and profit cannot coexist. But that thinking does not serve you, and it certainly does not serve your community. You cannot lead from exhaustion.

If you are delivering projects funded by grants, those projects are time-limited. That means you pay yourself as a self-employed freelancer or through your own limited company, invoicing your CIC for the hours you have worked. You are not paid a director's wage simply for being a director. You are paid for the work you do: project delivery, management, administration, training or facilitation, just like any other contractor.

When you invoice your CIC, include the hours you have worked, the rate agreed in the grant budget, and the name of the funder and project. Funders often ask for copies of invoices and bank statements to check that everything matches the budget you submitted. It should all align: the same figures, the same names, no surprises. If anything changes, go back to the funder for written approval before spending differently.

Whether you invoice from a sole trader business or a limited company is up to you. These days, there is little tax difference for most small operations. What matters is that your CIC setup is legitimate and transparent, paying for real work at fair market rates - and that it *looks* it, too.

Financial Confidence and Getting Paid Fairly

Many founders of community projects start from a place of service and care deeply about what they do. That makes money one of the hardest topics for them, and it becomes easy for them to undervalue their time. But a Community Interest Company has to be sustainable. That means you must treat money with the same respect you give your mission.

A CIC is not about personal profit, but that does not mean you should work for free. You deserve to be paid fairly for your time and your skills. Every strong CIC recognises that financial health and community impact go hand in hand. You cannot support others if you are constantly running on empty.

When you plan your projects, start with realistic pay. If you want to earn a decent income, focus on funders who pay professional rates. The Heritage Lottery Fund and Arts Council England are good examples. They typically pay day rates of around £350, sometimes higher for specialist roles, which allows you to deliver quality work and still cover your costs.

Other funders, like the National Lottery Community Fund or Sport England, might only pay hourly rates for instructors and will not always cover management time. There is nothing wrong with that, but you need to plan around it. Decide what kind of lifestyle and workload you want, then target the funding streams that match it. Some projects will pay less but require fewer hours. Others pay more but expect detailed delivery and reporting. Choose the mix that suits your reality.

Do not fall into the trap of pricing yourself like an employee. You are not being paid by the hour alone. You are running a project that involves preparation, coordination, delivery and admin. When you cost a project, think more like a freelancer or consultant. Funders will also want you to separate out project costs like materials and venue costs. Do factor in planning time, and all the hidden hours that make the work possible. For example, if the workshop is three hours long, charge a day rate, because the rest of the time will be spent doing project coordination and prep work.

Typical Project Pay Rates

Rates vary quite significantly depending on the funder.

To set expectations, here is a simple guide I give new founders.

- One of the lowest payers is Local Authority or HAF funding, often around minimum wage for direct delivery roles.
- National Lottery Community Fund, roughly £25 per hour for delivery roles, commonly budgeted at £150 per day.
- Heritage Lottery Fund or Arts Council England, £350 to £600 per day for project management and lead facilitators/artists, depending on expertise and responsibility.
- Sport England will pay £40 for an instructor facilitator. They won't pay for a project manager or coordinator at all.

The key is not to overwork yourself on underfunded projects. Respect your own time and value. If a project only pays minimum wage but aligns closely with your mission or raises your profile, treat it as a stepping stone. Use it to open doors to higher-paid work later.

When Income Is not From Grants

Not all income comes from funders. Your CIC can fundraise and trade, sell products, deliver workshops, run training, publish books or offer memberships. When the income does not come from grants, you can pay yourself whatever is fair under national pay standards. Freelancers in the UK typically charge between £350 and £600 a day, depending on experience. If your CIC earns money through trading, you can absolutely pay yourself within that range. Make sure it is proportionate to your workload and properly documented.

Trading income gives you freedom, stability and ownership. It means you can say no to underfunded projects and still pay your bills. It puts your mission back in your hands, not in a funder's. If you sell physical or creative products, such as artwork, books or courses, calculate all the time and materials involved before setting prices. Your pay should reflect the hours you have put in, not just the sale value.

Grants are brilliant for growth, but they are unpredictable. Over time, the goal is to rely less on grants and more on trading.

Balancing CIC and Personal Business

Most social entrepreneurs run a CIC and a separate business, either as a sole trader or a limited company. That is smart. It keeps your community work and your personal income balanced.

Your CIC is the place for grant funding and community projects. Your personal business is where you sell professional services, courses, books or products for profit. You can even license your own intellectual property to your CIC. For instance, you might let your CIC use a training programme or course you have created. That way, both sides benefit, and everything stays transparent.

Too many founders hide behind their CIC and neglect their own financial security. Then they burn out. When your personal business is financially healthy, it protects your CIC because it protects *you*. It keeps you creative, motivated and independent.

I coach CIC owners to build lasting, sustainable and simple social enterprise businesses alongside their CICs. From experience, I know how amazing it is to have a social enterprise with limitless income and impact. My CIC Tribe Ltd is an example of this. It has huge impact with no restrictions from funders. I raise funds through sales alone and still have an incredible social impact.

Purpose-driven people like you and me may not be natural salespeople. But with the right systems and design, you can have a thriving, successful, profit-making social enterprise that could even fund your CIC. My CIC Tribe Ltd donates some funds into our Oberi Art CIC. This has paid for that CIC's rent and overheads. We do not have to gain grants. We have great freedom to do as we please without the bother of grant funding, which is liberating.

I am passionate about helping social entrepreneurs to run simple businesses that take up minimal time and still give limitless impact and income. I think this is best achieved in an online business with automations and passive income. I help people set this up on my Purpose Plan online course **www.kellycoles.co.uk/purpose**. With my One Monday Month Method, this business can be maintained by working just one day a month to update and schedule whilst also using Meta Ads.

An example of this was my student Mat, who built a great CIC, Active Fitness CIC, after doing my online course 'How to set up a CIC and get funded fast'. He gained £140K in grant funding and started getting great results from fund-raising. He started to prefer fundraising, so I suggested that he put everything he knows about fundraising into an online course and a free download document called '100 fundraising ideas'. I designed a website for him and told him how to brand it. Boom: he launched and is now selling on automation. This is an easy social enterprise limited company that will run in the background to earn income and have a huge social impact so he can focus on his CIC work.

Simple ideas really work.

Getting the Right Help

It is worth finding an accountant who understands CICs properly. Many do not. A good one will save you stress and keep you compliant without costing the earth. Ask others in the CIC community for recommendations or look for professionals who specialise in social enterprise finance.

Before you hire anyone, ask them the simple question of how many CIC accounts they have handled. You want someone who understands deferred grant income, restricted funds, and the difference between trading surplus and profit. An accountant who knows the rules will protect you from unnecessary stress, penalties and lost money.

If they try to tell you to hire yourself PAYE on your CIC, run for the hills! This is a common mistake made by accountants. They want you to employ yourself PAYE, as that is both easy and profitable for them. But for you, it's fraud! A grant funder would breach your grant agreement and get very annoyed if they find you have been lumping their grant money for your freelancer pay into an employed paycheck. That will not be in the terms they agreed to. You can't just lob all the grants you get into one paycheck. You need to invoice for each grant project separately with clear paper trails, which you will be required to give to the grant funder after the project.

Employment also triggers Employer National Insurance, which a grant funder has not granted. The accountant should know this, yet many advise CICs incorrectly. Tell them you are a freelancer hired by your CIC, and that's the end of it. So, beware of accountants who give bad advice.

Record Keeping and Deferred Income

Another essential part of financial confidence is record-keeping. Every CIC should have a clear accounting system and a professional accountant. Never try to handle CIC accounts entirely on your own. The structure is different from standard business accounting, and errors can cause serious problems.

The biggest mistake I see is accountants who treat CIC funds as if they were profit. For example, if you have unspent grant money in your bank account at the end of the year, a general accountant might list it as taxable income. That is wrong. It is deferred grant funding allocated for specific costs, not profit. If you pay corporation tax on that money, you could breach your grant agreement.

Keep good habits too. Store receipts and invoices in one place, use a bookkeeping app if it helps, and stay on top of your reports. It might feel dull, but it is the difference between feeling in control and being constantly behind. Some funders will also ask to see your budgets, quotes and financial plans before awarding money. Treat that process as part of the job, not an obstacle. The more professional your financial documents look, the more seriously funders will take you.

You should also have a shared file with your directors, containing all your bank statements and invoices. They should have access, and they need to know where these are, should anything happen to you. I have had students who have suffered a stroke or concussion, and the directors have not had access to the files. The grant funders will expect the directors to have the information and will not be sympathetic if they say they don't have access.

Keeping a good system actually reduces your stress. Having organised shared systems keeps you on track and helps you stay compliant. When the funders ask to see things, you will not feel anxiety or panic.

Building Sustainable Income Streams

Once your foundation is solid, it is time to think about the future. A thriving CIC has more than one income stream. You might sell online courses or creative resources, launch a paid membership for your community, offer consultancy, mentoring or training, or create digital products and host ticketed events.

Even small recurring income makes a big difference. A ten-pound-a-month membership with one hundred members gives you one thousand pounds of predictable income before you even start applying for grants. An online course could be a recorded workshop series. A digital download might be a workbook that supports your community between sessions. Think of it as packaging your expertise in ways that keep giving, even when you are not in the room.

Think also about merchandise and paid events. The beauty of a CIC is that you have the opportunity to sell goods and services.

This is how you future-proof your CIC: build systems that generate income whether or not a funder says yes.

Telling the Financial Story

Good funders do not just want numbers. They want to understand your story behind them. When you write reports or applications, explain not only what you spent, but what those pounds achieved. What difference did that ten thousand pounds make? Who did it reach? What changed as a result?

Learning to tell the story behind your figures makes your reporting powerful. It turns data into evidence and evidence into new funding.

Setting Your Long-Term Financial Vision

Do not just think about survival. Think about sustainability. Yes, you might want to pay off debts or leave a job right now, but do not sacrifice your long-term wellbeing to do it.

Ask yourself these questions:

- What do I want my income to look like in five years?
- How many hours do I want to work?
- What kind of projects do I want to lead?

Financial freedom is not about earning endlessly. It is about having choice: choosing your projects, choosing your hours and choosing how you live. You are not just building a business model. You are designing a lifestyle that aligns with your purpose.

Money does not have to feel cold or corporate. It is simply energy, a resource that allows you to do more of what matters. When you start to see it that way, everything shifts. Earning stops feeling selfish. It becomes *service*, because the more sustainable you are, the more people you can help.

In Summary

Money does not have to be a mystery. Once you understand how to structure your pay, balance your income streams and plan for the future, it stops being stressful and becomes empowering.

Financial confidence is not about greed. It is about freedom. It is the difference between scraping by and standing tall. You are not just running a company; you are building a vehicle for change. And the stronger its engine, the further you can go.

Reflection:

- What worries you about CIC income?
- What are your money goals?
- What are your ideas for CIC income apart from grants?

Exercise:

Choose three income streams and make a plan of action. Think about short- and long-term goals.

7

Grant Funding and the Art of Resilience

When I applied for my first grant, I had no idea what I was doing. I spent hours trying to sound professional, using every phrase I thought funders wanted to hear. It got rejected in two weeks. The second time, I wrote it in plain English and spoke from the heart about what I wanted to do and why it mattered. That one got funded.

That was when I realised the system was not broken. I just needed to be clever with my wording.

Grant funding feels intimidating until you understand how it works. Once you do, it becomes one of the most empowering tools you will ever learn, because when you can confidently find and secure funding, you can turn your ideas into reality.

You have built your CIC, you have got structure, presence and a sense of purpose. Now comes the part that turns dreams into delivery: securing the money to make it happen.

Where Funding Really Comes From

There are far more opportunities out there than most people realise. Grants come from councils, community foundations, charitable trusts, corporate sponsors, national lotteries, even universities and health boards.

Each has its own priorities and personality. Local councils often fund community cohesion projects: things that bring residents together, support young people, or improve wellbeing. National Lottery funding is wide-ranging, focusing on projects that tackle disadvantage or strengthen communities. Charitable trusts might back niche causes such as mental health, arts, heritage or education. Corporate foundations like Aviva, Gatwick Airport and Tesco fund projects that align with their social values.

Understanding where your CIC fits within this landscape is half the battle. You are not trying to be everything to everyone. You are trying to find the funders who believe in your idea. The trick is to match your mission to their priorities. If your project aligns with their goals, your chances of success rise dramatically. It is not about luck. It is about alignment with the funder's priorities.

Finding and Securing Grant Funding

Grant funding is the lifeblood of many Community Interest Companies. It gives you the resources to turn your ideas into real projects without taking on debt or personal risk. But while funding can open doors, finding the right grants and writing successful applications takes patience, strategy and persistence.

Start with a simple search. Type your cause alongside the word 'funding'. Be specific. If you support mental health, search for 'mental health grant funding UK'. You will be surprised by how many results appear. Look at both national and local options and keep a running list of anything that seems relevant.

Next, contact your local community foundation. Every region in the UK has one, and each foundation manages a collection of local grants. These are often smaller pots of money, but they are usually easier to apply for and can help you build a track record.

After that, speak to your local council or MP's office. Many councils have small grant schemes or can point you towards upcoming opportunities. Councillors and community officers often know when new funding is due to be released.

Then move to the national funders. The National Lottery Community Fund, otherwise known as Awards for All, is one of the most commonly received grants, covering a wide range of themes including health, wellbeing, environment and inclusion. Sport England, Arts Council England and the Heritage Lottery Fund also have their own focus areas. Look carefully at their priorities and think about how your idea fits.

One of the biggest secrets in grant funding is the power of pivoting. If you can adapt your project slightly to match a funder's aims, you will have far more opportunities. For example, if you run a women's support group, you might design a physical activity project for Sport England, an art-based project for Arts Council England, or a nature-based one for the Heritage Lottery Fund. Each version still serves your mission but meets a different funder's goals. The more flexible you are, the more doors open.

When writing grants, think about *Who, What, Where, When* and *How.* Always add the details like how many will attend, how long the session is, and how many sessions. The most common reason for rejection is that people just forget to add crucial details.

Many grant applications ask you for a project plan or schedule. This does not have to be intimidating. Funders simply want to see that you have planned your project well, how you will deliver your project, and how you will measure its success. Keep your plan detailed but realistic. List your sessions, your timeline and the outcomes you expect. Always base your costs on real quotes or previous experience, not rough guesses.

The time it takes to hear back from a funder varies. Most applications are reviewed within four to twelve weeks, but some take longer. The key is to plan ahead and never rely on one single application. Treat grant writing like planting seeds. Some take root quickly, others take time, and a few do not grow at all.

Rejection is part of the process. Even strong applications can be turned down for reasons beyond your control. Always ask for feedback. Most major funders allow you to reapply immediately after making the recommended changes. Often, it takes just one or two rounds of feedback to succeed. Each attempt teaches you something that makes the next application stronger.

With experience, you will start to recognise patterns. You will see which funders align best with your work, which questions come up repeatedly, and what language seems to resonate. You will begin to develop a rhythm, an instinct for what makes an application sing.

One of the most valuable lessons is learning not to take rejections personally. They are not a reflection of your worth or your project's potential. They are simply part of the landscape. The people who succeed with grant funding are not necessarily the most experienced. They are the ones who keep going.

Finally, celebrate your wins, no matter how small. The first successful grant you receive changes everything. It validates your idea, boosts your confidence, and often opens the door to more opportunities. Funders trust success. Once you have delivered one good project, others follow more easily.

Grant funding is a skill, one that you can learn, practise and master. It is not luck. The more you understand the system, the more control you have over your CIC's future. So keep learning, keep applying and never stop refining. Each application is another step towards the impact you want to make.

The Emotional Journey of Applying

For many founders, applying for funding is an emotional process. There is pride, fear, excitement and often a bit of imposter syndrome. You might worry that you are not official enough, that you do not know the right words, or that someone else will do it better.

I promise you that is not true.

Funders are not looking for perfection. They are looking for people who genuinely care and who can show that care through organised, thoughtful planning. They want to see that your CIC is real, that you have a handle on your budget and that you are committed to making a difference.

Your first few applications might feel clumsy. That is fine. Everyone starts there. The important thing is to start.

What Funders Actually Want

It is easy to overthink what funders expect. In reality, they are looking for a few simple things:

1. A clear purpose. What are you trying to achieve and for whom?
2. Evidence of need. Show that people want or need your work. Use surveys, feedback, statistics or stories.
3. A realistic plan. Break down what you will do, when and how.
4. A fair budget. Do not underprice yourself. They expect you to pay yourself and your team.
5. Impact measurement. Explain how you will know if it is working.

Above all, they want confidence – not ego, but reliability. They need to trust that if they give you money, you will deliver what you have promised.

The Power of Plain English

Grant assessors see hundreds of applications, so make yours really clear and bold. The first two sentences should be dramatic and exciting. I have heard that assessors stop reading if the first two sentences do not grab their attention.

Next, break the answers down. You will notice that applications often make bullet-pointed suggestions of what they want you to cover in your answers to the questions. Hit each of these points in a clear, short paragraph.

Assessors are not English teachers. They do not care about a bit of bad grammar and spelling within reason. You can use AI to tidy up your answers and make them look better, but do not rely on AI too much, as it will do a terrible job on its own, and the assessor will be able to tell if it's just some AI rubbish. So, write your answer first, include all the details you need, then put it through AI.

It is a good idea to slot in a few terms from the website of the grant funder. They publish their strategies and priorities, so use these terms. For example, Awards for All prioritises the cost-of-living crisis. You might say, "This project clearly meets the priority of the cost-of-living crisis by giving free food and a warm space to 200 low-income families." Hit one of their clear priorities with a *measurable outcome*.

Dealing With Rejection

Let us be honest. You will get rejected. Everyone does. It does not mean your idea was bad or that you are not good enough. It simply means your project did not fit that particular fund at that particular time.

Sometimes, it is about timing. Sometimes, there were too many applicants. Sometimes, they just did not have enough money to go around. Other times, they wanted to give it to you, but they needed you to tighten up a few aspects of the project application.

When that happens, do not spiral. Ask for feedback. Funders are usually happy to tell you why you did not get through, and their advice is gold dust for your next application. The major funders give you feedback and the opportunity to resubmit. You can also make a freedom of information request to see your panel results, scoring and information on who was successful. I have done this with many of my clients for Arts Council England. Charlotte was one of them after her first application was rejected. We found out the scoring and saw she was very close. So, we tweaked the application based on this information, and she was successful on the second submission for £30,000. This was for a brand-new (non-arts) CIC that was pivoting into a photography project to document women in sport.

Treat applying like a numbers game. Charlotte applied for twenty grants in year one and got five, totalling £67k. The accepted ones were all major national funders. This was because the national pots are so much easier to get. Local grants often have small pots, the funds run out quickly, and you can't reapply.

Case Studies: Real People, Real Funding

Hamzah of Cricket Arena CIC applied for forty-five grants in just over a year after completing my course. He understood it was a numbers game and rejection isn't to be feared. He won sixteen out of the forty-five. His attitude kept him applying until he had sufficient for his CIC – a third of what he applied for. He kept re-applying and didn't quit. You have to learn to keep going.

Building Relationships With Funders

When you get funding, nurture that relationship. Send updates, photos and thank you notes if you are given a project manager. Most people make limited contact with their funders.

As a rule, make sure you post on social media and tag the funder if appropriate. Create a footprint on socials throughout the project, as they will go back and check. Let them see their money in action.

When a project ends, report back honestly. If something did not go to plan, explain what you learned. Be confident and emphasise the positives of any planned changes. Things change, which is ok, but always present them with a solution. You don't want to flag yourself as a risk or trigger an audit check. Try to stay under the radar. Stick to your project plan and budgets, and if you need to change anything, email them first to ask. Save their agreement and keep it as evidence.

A simple thank you message or short update can lead to years of repeat support. It is that human connection that builds trust.

Showing Impact

Impact is how you prove that your work is working. It is not just about numbers. It is about change.

Show before and after stories. Capture voices, faces (when you have consent) and moments of transformation. Funders love seeing evidence that their investment created tangible results.

You might be able to say: *Eighty-five per cent of participants reported improved confidence after our course. One said, "I feel like I finally belong somewhere."*

That mix of data and humanity is unbeatable.

Social impact is measured by outcomes achieved. One great way is to work out what you achieved for every £1 raised. Make infographics to visually capture your stats. You could have a food graphic and next to it write '1000 free meals distributed'. You can make these in Canva: no need to pay anyone. These are great for your website and social media posts.

Sometimes we find it hard to boast about what we do. Do not be shy, because it is important to make clear the difference your CIC makes to people. You are likely to be creating impact in more ways than you think. Sometimes it is best to find out all the ways the project helped your participants by interviewing them.

Keep all your evidence organised. Create folders for photos, testimonials, reports and statistics. You will use them in future applications and marketing. Your impact archive will become your CIC's most powerful selling tool.

Ethical Storytelling

When sharing impact, always tell stories respectfully and protect people's dignity and privacy. Ask for permission before sharing photos or quotes. You will need a privacy policy and signed consent forms for all media and gain permission before sharing anything. Even if some individuals do not give permission, you can still get lots of content, such as audio, photos of hands doing things, leaving out faces.

Focus on empowerment of the people who benefit from your CIC, not pity. Also, don't use stigmatising language. For example, instead of saying 'mental health project' describe it as a 'wellbeing activity'. Instead of 'debt management workshops' say 'financial growth workshops'. Instead of 'soup kitchen' call it a 'community food share'.

Instead of showing people at their lowest, highlight the strength they find through your work. It shows integrity, compassion and professionalism, and funders notice this. When people trust you with their stories, treat that as the privilege it is.

Learning the Rhythm of Funding

Funding has its own rhythm. Some opportunities are open all year, while others appear seasonally. Once you have applied for a few, you will start to recognise patterns: which funders are quick, which are slow, and which ones fit your projects best.

Build a funding calendar. Create a simple spreadsheet with deadlines and decision dates, amounts available, eligibility notes and contact names. Plan six months ahead so you never have to scramble. Overlap project timelines so when one ends, another begins. That is how sustainable CIC's stay funded year-round.

Remember not to burn yourself out on delivery and leave time to grow your non-grant funding options. Use volunteers and other staff to help you cover your grant-funded projects.

As your grant funding pipeline grows, your confidence and experience will also. You will learn which grant projects you liked and which you might not apply for again. It is common for people to apply for the most grants in years one and two, but to become more choosy after that and only go for grants they really like running. After year two, you will probably be fundraising and have other income. Being grant-funded is not the end game; it's the growth period.

The Funding Mindset

Winning funding is partly skill, partly mindset. You need resilience to handle the 'no' and curiosity to keep learning. The founders who succeed are not the most polished or experienced. They are the ones who keep trying. They understand that rejection is not failure; it is feedback.

Grant writing is a conversation, not a test. Each bid helps you understand your own work more clearly. I find that rejection often makes for a much better project the second time around. It is not negative at all. The funder wants you to get the funding, remember!

With each success, you build belief in yourself. Over time, you stop feeling like an applicant and start feeling like a partner – someone bringing value to the table, not asking for a favour.

Building a Portfolio of Success

As your experience grows, you will find that one success leads to another. Funders love to back proven organisations.

Keep a simple portfolio of your wins. List each grant, amount, funder and project outcome. Add testimonials, photos and quotes. This becomes your evidence pack, something you can attach to new bids or send to potential partners.

A professional, well-documented portfolio sets you apart immediately. It shows you are serious, consistent and capable. Before long, funders will start coming to you.

An example of this is from my own CIC projects. I always added a zine (a small magazine, like a booklet) to record every exhibition I did. This has built up to a wonderful range of books I can use to showcase my project work. I have also published a few YouTube presentations from Heritage Lottery Research, which are nice and easy to share if I need to. Easy, shareable videos and downloads in your portfolio are great. You can use them to gain more funding or contract work. You could even grow a career from them as a speaker, writer, historian, artist, etc.

One of the major benefits of a CIC is that you are given a big budget to show off your skills and work, and you can gain an incredible portfolio. You are given the budget to hire incredible professionals to work with you, and to hire and buy venues and equipment. You can even gain training on the project. This can have more power than many degrees to open new career doors.

Beyond Grants

While grants are powerful, they are not the only way to grow. Many successful CICs blend grant funding with fundraising, paid contracts, sponsorships and trading income.

Grants help you get started. Trading gives you freedom. Contracts give you stability. Together, they build long-term sustainability.

That is where we are heading next.

In Summary

Grant funding is not a mystery. It is a skill, a rhythm and an attitude.

Be clear. Be human. Be persistent.

Every application teaches you something. Every project strengthens your reputation. Every success builds the kind of resilience that makes your CIC unstoppable.

Because funding is not just about money. It is about belief. When someone funds your project, they are saying, “We believe in you.”

And when you learn to believe in yourself with the same conviction, that is when your impact really begins.

Reflection:

- Which types of funders do you feel most aligned with?
- How do you usually respond when a grant is rejected?
- What does resilience mean to you in your funding journey?
- How could you make your next application feel more human and authentic?

Exercise:

1. Choose three funders that align with your CIC’s mission. Write down why each is a good fit.
2. Draft a 150-word project summary in plain English.
3. Create a simple funding tracker with deadlines, outcomes and next steps.
4. After your next application, review how the process felt and note one thing you will do differently next time.

Optional Resource List

The National Lottery Community Fund

Arts Council England

Sport England

The Aviva Community Fund

The National Emergencies Trust

Local Community Foundations (search your area + 'Community Foundation')

BBC Children in Need

The Joseph Rowntree Charitable Trust

All have funded CICs across the UK, from grassroots groups to national movements.

8

Contracts, Commissions and the Power of Partnership

After you have mastered grant funding, a new question arises. What comes next? You have proven your impact, you have built relationships, and suddenly doors begin to open. This is when your CIC steps into its next chapter: the point at which people not only believe in your idea but trust in your ability to deliver it.

If grant funding is the heartbeat of your CIC, contracts are its backbone. They bring stability, credibility and continuity. Through them, small community projects grow into established providers, recognised by local authorities, schools, the NHS and national organisations.

When you start winning contracts, you move from short-term survival to long-term sustainability. It is not just a financial shift; it is an identity shift. You stop being a project runner and start being a recognised provider, a partner that institutions rely on.

What Contracts Actually Are

Let us strip away the jargon. A contract is simply an agreement that says, "We will deliver this service, and you will pay us for it."

It might mean:

- A council paying you to run youth mentoring or wellbeing workshops.
- A school commissioning you to deliver an arts or sports programme.
- The NHS contracting your CIC to provide health education or community engagement.

A grant funds your idea because it has potential. A contract pays you because you have already proved your reliability. It is about trust and evidence. Once your CIC reaches this stage, your work gains weight. You are no longer pitching for belief; you are being paid for delivery.

Why Contracts Matter

Something changes when your CIC wins its first contract. It is not just about the money. It is about legitimacy. You move from being a local doer of good things to being recognised as a professional provider.

That moment shifts how others see you, and how you see yourself. Partners treat you differently. Your voice carries more weight in meetings. You become part of the system that delivers change, not just someone shouting from the sidelines.

Contracts bring consistency. They let you plan ahead, hire staff and develop services instead of constantly chasing the next pot of funding. They allow you to grow with confidence. It is not a departure from purpose; it is an evolution of it.

Understanding Procurement

Public sector organisations, like councils and the NHS, award most contracts through a process called procurement. This is how they make sure suppliers are chosen fairly and transparently.

You will see opportunities advertised on sites such as:

- Contracts Finder
- Find a Tender
- Proactis or Delta eSourcing (portals used by many councils)
- NHS Supply Chain

In addition to looking at those sites, in order to sell to the prison service or the Department of Work and Pensions (Jobcentre), you need to be on the Baseware system.

I have successfully done this before. I used a community fund grant to run a pilot project in a local prison to design and build a rehabilitation course that prisoners could take in their cells. Fully funded by that grant, I developed the course. I then sold it to the same prison in bulk batches of fifty prisoners receiving the in-cell self-study courses for £7000. After the first sale and with great reviews, I was then able to sell this to several other prisons through the Baseware system. This is a great example of how to use grant funding to develop a product or service you later sell, which moves your CIC towards sustainability with little to no original investment.

Each notice outlines what they want, how to apply, and the deadline. These systems are not just for big companies. Many CICs win tenders every year because they offer something larger organisations cannot: authenticity, local knowledge and trust within the community.

Getting Ready for Contracts

Before you apply, get contract-ready. You do not need a large office or a big staff team. You do need the basics that show commissioners you are professional and prepared.

- Strong governance: Keep safeguarding, data protection, equality and diversity, and health and safety policies up to date.
- Insurance: Public liability and professional indemnity are usually required.
- A proven track record: Even small projects count. Show what you delivered and what changed as a result.
- References. Gather testimonials from funders, schools or partner organisations.
- Financial clarity: Keep accounts tidy and transparent.

This is all about demonstrating social impact and good value for money, especially with state-run departments. Use clear infographics showing impact and write social impact reports. You can hire a specialist to write you a great social impact report.

Treat every grant as a pilot for future commissions. Run a simple mock tender for practice. Describe your service in 250 words, sketch a budget and list your outcomes. Clarity builds confidence.

Finding the Right Opportunities

Contracts are everywhere once you know where to look. Local councils commission holiday schemes, after-school clubs, youth mentoring and community wellbeing. NHS trusts commission social prescribing, health education and mental health support. Housing associations and universities commission outreach, training and engagement. Private companies sometimes commission CICs to meet their social value commitments.

Register yourself on ProContract **https://procontract.due-north.com/Login**, which is a great site to get contracts with all of the above-listed organisations. These organisations put out bid jobs for different things, perhaps some research, a workshop or a street art mural. You can get some quite obscure, exciting projects listed. In our local area, there was an old toilet block in some woods. The fund offered a £20,000 grant to refurbish the block and do some kind of art project there. If you get something like this, you also get given a building, land and a grant.

Do not chase everything. Focus on work that fits your mission and capacity. Ask yourself if this contract helps your CIC do more of what it is here for. That single question keeps your growth aligned and sustainable.

The Power of Relationships

Many successful contracts start with a conversation. Meet people. Attend local forums and partnership meetings. Introduce yourself to community leads, procurement officers and commissioners. Tell them what your CIC does and, more importantly, listen to what they need.

When decision makers know who you are, you are not just another name in a tender list. You are a person they trust. One music facilitator I worked with began by volunteering at a youth centre. A year later, the council commissioned weekly workshops as part of their youth engagement strategy. It was not luck. It was visibility, trust and follow-through.

You should get yourself well known among the local councillors, MPs and Mayors, plus the local police and crime commission. This can really pay off in terms of references from them... and photo opportunities can keep them sweet. Start with an open day and invite them down.

Relationships create contracts faster than paperwork ever can.

What Commissioners Really Look For

After many conversations with commissioners, a pattern appears of what they want:

- Clear and quick communication.
- Flexibility when things change.
- Honesty over polish. If something slips, say so early and offer a solution.
- Partners who make their jobs easier.

More than anything, a relationship with a commissioner is about money and what clear and deliverable outcomes you will create.

Here is a great example. Julian runs a CIC for dads and a project to help counsel fathers who have suffered baby loss. He travels the country talking to NHS Trusts. He has convinced many to give him a year-long contract that pays for him to deliver the project. After that, the deal is that the men in the group will fundraise to pay for the next cohort of men. This pay it forward model is very attractive to the NHS as they get a free service after the first year.

Commissioners are human. They want reliable, impactful, value-for-money services that make their jobs easier, serve their beneficiaries and make them look good. Give them an offer they can't refuse.

Contracts, Partnerships and Protecting Your Work

As your CIC develops, your relationships with other organisations, freelancers and venues become more complex. This is where clear contracts protect the quality of your work.

A good contract is a plain English agreement that covers three essentials:

- Timeline. When the work will happen.
- Deliverables. What exactly will be delivered.
- Payment. How and when you will be paid.

Never rely on verbal promises, even with people you trust. Details get lost, and memories differ. Written agreements create accountability on both sides.

Agree payment terms before any work begins. For larger projects, staged payments work well, for example, on signing, mid-project and on completion. This keeps cash flow healthy for you and reassurance high for partners.

Beware of the state services suddenly backtracking and not having the money. Things change fast, and staff change regularly, creating an unstable system to work with. Because of that, never start working before you get paid. I once spent a month or more working on a programme for the police, only for them to change their minds after I had designed the programme. I have also had NHS staff tell me there is funding, and the day before the project is due to start, a new staff member tells me the other guy has evaporated, and there is no money. It can be frustrating, so that is why you need contracts and to be paid upfront.

Life happens. Venues close, a freelancer becomes unwell, equipment fails. Tell your funder or commissioner as soon as anything significant changes. Explain clearly, propose a replacement plan, and ask for written approval before you alter delivery. This transparency builds trust that lasts beyond a single project.

Pricing Your Services

Budgets in schools and councils are tight, but do not undersell yourself. You are not selling a few hours. You are pricing in preparation, coordination, materials and overheads. A realistic guide for a professional CIC facilitator is around £600 per day, or £300 for a half day. Holding that line keeps the work sustainable and the quality high. It is fine to say no when a price does not reflect the real cost.

I had two ladies who were employed in a school as councillors. They designed and delivered great group work for the children. They decided to quit and start a CIC. They sold that same service back to the same school for three times their wages. That is because when you become a freelancer, you need to triple your fee as a normal wage does not cover all the business costs. This isn't extortion: in fact, it is often cheaper for the school or organisation to hire you this way rather than employ you. Employing people can be risky and expensive overall.

If an organisation tries to bring you in on a wage rate, tell them you are not accepting an employee wage, because you are a business with overheads that need to be included in your fee or what you offer would be unsustainable.

Safeguards With Partners and Freelancers

When hiring others as freelancers on projects, make sure you have some safeguards in place to protect yourself. You will need to hire people for a variety of roles, such as media, marketing, delivery and services.

When hiring venues or partnering with people, always have a backup plan. Identify an alternative venue, a second practitioner or a partner CIC before you start. Never pay freelancers upfront – what if they get sick or are unable to attend for some other reason? You can pay yourself in advance for management time because you know you will deliver. For others, use staged payments linked to milestones. If someone fails to deliver after being paid, the obligation to fix it rests with you, not the funder. Good agreements prevent that headache.

Case Study: From Grant to Contract

A CIC supporting young fathers, Dads Pads CIC, began with a £10,000 grant to run parenting workshops. They delivered well, captured testimonials and measured outcomes. They then shared their results with the local NHS trust. Impressed by the evidence, the trust commissioned a fatherhood app that reached hundreds of families. The contract paid more than £400,000 a year. This did not happen overnight. It came from treating every grant as a pilot, proving impact and staying professional.

Case Study:
Creativity Meets Commissioning

A music project in London, Karlee Training, accredited a musical and media course aimed at kids in school who wouldn't be doing a GCSE, often those with SEND or at risk of exclusion. The school paid £27k per year on a BACS payment. This CIC was then able to roll this model out to many schools across London. Getting a course accredited was key: it meant this became a no-brainer for the school, as they would be able to pull down funding because they kept those children in school, and they still got some kind of a qualification even though they could not give them a GCSE. This CIC's turnover for these contracts is £90k a year.

Delivering With Excellence

Winning a contract is one thing. Delivering it well earns your reputation. Read the agreement carefully. Know the outcomes expected, reporting dates and success measures.

Meet or exceed the targets. Keep records, send brief updates, and if a problem arises, do not hide it. Offer a fix.

Reliability becomes your greatest asset. That is how one contract turns into five.

Building a Team and Scaling Up

As you grow, bring in sessional staff, subcontractors or volunteers. You can also partner with other CICs to deliver larger programmes. Be clear about roles and finance. Put agreements in writing. Collaboration creates credibility and spreads the workload.

My Own Journey With Contracts

When I first looked at contracts, I thought they were only for bigger organisations. Then, a local prison asked me to deliver personal development workshops. I said yes, nervous but determined. It became one of the most meaningful experiences of my career and led to other commissions. I learned that the difference between a small CIC and a large provider is often confidence and preparation. Offering pilots and evidence is key. Ensuring that you consult the community that will benefit from the project is also key. The funder or commissioner wants to see that the community is involved in the design. When I did my prison rehabilitation project, the prisoners' feedback and evidence that the project had made a difference to their lives was key in helping me design the final version. Convincing managers to let go of money means you have to prove there is a demand.

Understanding Social Value

You will often see the term 'social value' in tenders. This means the extra benefit your organisation brings beyond the contract. That could be hiring locally, offering free community sessions, using eco-friendly materials, or providing training opportunities. CICs excel here because community impact is already at your core. Make sure you highlight it. Again, make your infographics and eye-catching results easy to read. Make the impact jump out.

The Rhythm of Procurement

Procurement has its own rhythm. Some contracts are annual; others are open all year. Keep an opportunity calendar with deadlines, decision dates, contract lengths and reporting requirements. Start with small local opportunities, often under £10,000, with simpler applications. As your experience grows, move into larger frameworks and regional tenders. Plan to overlap the delivery of projects so your income remains steady.

Turning Contracts Into Partnerships

Deliver a few contracts well and something important happens. You become the organisation people call first. Commissioners prefer to work with those they trust. If you have a reputation for reliability and care, new work often arrives directly. One founder I mentor began with a single local council project. Now her CIC delivers wellbeing sessions for three NHS trusts. Each began as a small pilot. Her secret was simple: she did what she said she would, every time.

Bringing It All Together

Contracts and commissions are not the end of your journey. They are the evolution of it. They turn purpose into permanence. Start small. Stay consistent. Keep learning. Each project is a stepping stone to greater trust and bigger opportunities. You do not need to be corporate. You do need to be confident.

In Summary

Contracts bring structure, stability and respect to the work you already love doing. They open doors to partnerships, growth and sustainability. When you started your CIC, it was an idea. Contracts turn that idea into a legacy. If grants gave you wings, contracts give you roots. Once you are rooted, you can grow in every direction.

Practical Toolkit

Useful places to look:

- Contracts Finder
- Find a Tender Service
- Local authority procurement portals
- NHS Supply Chain
- Social Enterprise UK guidance
- ProContract
- CIC Tribe resources for policy templates and bid examples

Keep this list nearby. Opportunities appear every week, and being ready is half the battle.

Reflection:

- Where could your current work translate directly into a paid service for a council, school or NHS team?
- Which two people could you introduce yourself to this month who influence commissioning locally?
- What parts of your delivery need tightening so that a commissioner would feel fully confident in you?

Exercise:

Create a one-page contract-ready pack.

1. Write a 200-word service summary in plain English.
2. List three outcomes you can evidence from recent work.
3. Add two short testimonials with names or roles.
4. Note your day rate or package price and what it includes.
5. Attach a simple checklist of your policies and insurance.

Send this pack to yourself as a PDF. It becomes your starting point for tender portals, warm emails to commissioners and partnership conversations.

9

Fundraising and the Art of Community Support

By now, you've learned how to apply for grants and even deliver contracts. Those are the big structural steps that give your CIC financial stability. But there's another income stream that's smaller, simpler and, in many ways, more personal – fundraising.

Fundraising is a powerful yet hugely overlooked income stream in CICs. People get so focused on the grants that they forget they can legally fundraise as a CIC. Fundraising is far better than grant funding, as these are unrestricted funds you can spend on what you want. No applications, no having to bend to their priorities, no evaluation paperwork. You can just get the cash and do your activities with it. You can pay salaries if you can raise enough regularly.

Every CIC should have a fundraising strategy that works on repeat and gives you recurring income. This does not have to be a lot of work when you get help from volunteers or sponsors.

Fundraising is a great way to engage your community, and this helps you build confidence and community social proof that leads to grants and contracts. It is not just about the total in the collection tin. It is about connections. It is about proving that people believe in what you're building, long before the big funders ever take notice.

Here is an inspiring example for you. Matt from Active Fitness CIC had a great first couple of CIC years, gaining over £150k in grants. But when he started fundraising, he decided this was far easier and more sustainable. Now, 40% of his CIC income is from fundraising.

Fundraising builds community around your mission. It raises awareness, strengthens relationships, and gives you flexible income you can use for anything from insurance to event costs. It is also empowering because it puts control back in your hands. You do not have to wait for approval from a funder; instead, you're inviting people to join your mission.

Starting From Zero

Not every CIC begins with a crowd of supporters or a long list of funders. Most start with one person and an idea. If you are at this point, your own circle of friends and family are often the start. You could start with a collection of clothes and toys for a pre-loved sale in the community. These can be great for gaining the first pounds for your setup costs.

As you get started with your grant-funded workshops, you can begin growing a community, and people will start offering to help. You will attract volunteers. If you nurture this, you can turn this support into fundraising income. People who want to support you can be encouraged to go on sponsored walks, runs, climbs, etc.

You can build in regular fundraising events like fairs, markets, talks, dinners, etc., selling tickets or hiring out stalls. These are great ways to fundraise. In my early CIC days, I ran wedding fairs that made around £1-3k each. I did ten over the year in different locations.

Sophie from Take a Deep Breath CIC, a wonderful community choir CIC, runs a quarterly wellbeing fair which turns over £4k plus, not to mention the community engagement and social proof numbers she gets from it. Having a fair is a multiple-bonus activity because you get to have your own stall at it from which to promote your CIC.

The Fundraising Mindset

Many founders feel awkward about asking for money. It can feel like begging, especially if you've never done it before. But fundraising isn't about asking for help. It is about offering hope.

You are not taking from people. You are giving people the chance to be part of something meaningful. People want to contribute to good things. They just need a cause to believe in and someone to ask them to help. When you see fundraising as inclusion rather than obligation, everything changes. You move from apology to confidence.

So next time you post a fundraiser or plan an event, don't lead with desperation. Lead with purpose. Say, "Here's what we're creating. Here's why it matters. Would you like to be part of it?" You will be amazed at how differently people respond when they sense genuine energy and belief.

Understanding Fundraising for CICs

CICs can fundraise legally and effectively even though they are not charities. You simply need to be transparent. If you run a CIC, you can absolutely raise money, but you must always make it clear that you are a Community Interest Company, not a charity. That means any campaign, collection or event should be clearly labelled with your CIC name and registration number.

Transparency protects you and your supporters. It shows integrity, builds trust and ensures that donors understand exactly who and what they're supporting.

At the start, keep things small and manageable. Focus on local, community-driven fundraising such as raffles, sales or small events. These can be done safely without formal registration. Once you've been operating for a year and have a few projects under your belt, you *must* register with the Fundraising Regulator, which oversees fundraising in the UK. This is a legal requirement.

Why Fundraising Matters

Fundraising isn't just about covering costs. It is a visibility tool. Every time someone donates, volunteers or shares your work, they become part of your story.

When you later apply for a grant or partnership, that community support becomes proof. Funders love to see grassroots momentum. It shows that your idea already has public backing.

Even small amounts of money can make a huge difference in your early days. A few hundred pounds can pay for insurance, venue hire or printing of materials. More importantly, it proves that you can generate income independently – that evidence strengthens every future funding bid.

Fundraising also builds pride. It reminds you that people believe in your work. It brings your CIC to life in your local area, turning it from a name on paper into something people feel connected to.

The Power of Storytelling

The secret to successful fundraising is storytelling. Facts tell, but stories sell. People rarely give to data. They give to emotion, purpose and people.

When you fundraise, talk about why your CIC exists. Use simple, heartfelt language. Show what change looks like. Share photos, short videos or quotes that capture real impact.

Keep it authentic. You don't need a marketing team. You just need honesty. A short, unpolished video of you explaining your mission will connect more deeply than a glossy campaign with no soul. Having CIC-branded T-shirts and buckets in group photos looks great. It looks like a solid community project.

And always close the loop. After the fundraiser ends, show what happened next. Post photos, updates and thank-yous. People love seeing the difference their contribution made. It builds lasting trust and sets you up for future success.

Getting Started:
Simple Fundraisers That Work

You don't need a big budget or a full team to fundraise effectively. Start small and start local.

If you're just beginning, look at what you already have. Many CIC founders raise their first few hundred pounds by selling items they no longer need. Platforms such as Vinted, eBay and Facebook Marketplace are quick ways to free up cash for registration fees or materials. You can even ask family or friends to donate items for resale. This is a low-pressure, low-risk way to generate income and start feeling in control.

Charity shops are often overwhelmed with donations, which means you can help reduce waste by collecting unwanted items and giving them new life through sales. A small online auction or pop-up sale is easy to run and creates a sense of shared purpose.

Once you've built a little traction, try community events and sponsored activities. A sponsored walk or local fun run gets people involved physically and emotionally. If ten people raise £100 each, that's £1,000 – enough to cover insurance or your next project.

Other options include:

- **Pre-loved sales** that raise money and bring people together.
- **Coffee mornings or raffles** that combine socialising with support.
- **Online shopping donations** using the Easy Fundraising app, which lets supporters raise small amounts every time they shop.

The key is to keep things simple, visible and joyful. Fundraising should feel like a celebration of what you're building, not a burden.

Easy Fundraising

My mention above of the Easy Fundraising app might be the first time you've heard of it. You register your CIC with the app, and then you get supporters, including yourself, to shop through it for everything they buy online – whether that's a holiday, their weekly online shop or their Amazon orders. If they buy through the Easy Fundraising app, you get lots of commission income donated to your CIC. Say you get twenty supporters and they each raise £300 a year on average: that's £6000 in a year. Great income.

My current CIC gains about £1000 every quarter from Easy Fundraising, and this pays for our CIC's van hire. It is a great way to fundraise easily. Perhaps you'd like to take a look: **www.easyfundraising.org.uk/cic-tribe**

Partnering With Businesses

Businesses often have small budgets for community engagement. Many will sponsor a local project, cover event costs or donate equipment in return for visibility and goodwill. Approach them with a simple one-page proposal outlining who you are, what your project does, what you need and how they'll be recognised.

Sponsorship doesn't just mean money. Sometimes it means free venue space, donated materials or professional expertise. Over time, these partnerships can grow into major collaborations.

Creating a Simple Fundraising Plan

Having a basic plan helps you stay focused and professional. Use this simple structure for each campaign:

1. Goal: What are you raising money for?
2. Target: How much do you need?
3. Timeframe: When will it happen?
4. Audience: Who will support you?
5. Promotion: How will you share it?
6. Follow-up: How will you thank supporters and report results?

Treat fundraising like a project. Plan it, track it, celebrate it. That professionalism sets your CIC apart.

Legal and Ethical Essentials

Transparency is everything. Always display your CIC name and registration number on donation materials. Be clear about how money will be used, keep full records, and follow Gambling Commission guidance for raffles or lotteries. Use secure platforms like PayPal, Square or SumUp for online donations.

If you're still in your first year, keep activity local and small-scale. Focus on community-based efforts until your registration with the Fundraising Regulator is complete. Ethical fundraising builds long-term trust and ensures supporters feel reassured that their contributions are used responsibly.

Overcoming the Fear of Asking

The hardest part of fundraising isn't logistics. It is mindset. Many of us carry old beliefs that asking for money is wrong or embarrassing. But the truth is, money is simply a tool for impact. Without it, your work can't reach the people who need it.

When you invite people to contribute, you're not burdening them. You are giving them a chance to align their resources with their values. Fundraising teaches humility and courage. It teaches you to trust that your cause is worthy - and shows you, time and again, that people are more generous than you think.

The Long Game

Once fundraising becomes part of your culture, it keeps your CIC thriving. Plan a yearly rhythm: small community events, one digital campaign and a few corporate sponsorships. Each one reinforces your visibility and credibility. Over time, you'll notice a shift. People won't just donate - they'll champion you.

Fundraising then stops feeling like work and starts feeling like community.

Reflection:

- Which story in this chapter resonated most with you and why?
- If you don't yet have supporters, how can you start building a community around your CIC?
- What is one small, meaningful way you could raise your first £100?
- How could you show your supporters the impact of their contributions?

Exercise

Write down five potential ways to raise funds over the next three months. For each, note how much you aim to raise, what the money will support, and who can help. Then create one small action plan to bring the first idea to life. Even the smallest win builds belief and momentum.

10

Building Sustainability and the Future of Your CIC

When I first started out, I thought success meant getting the next grant, the next project, the next 'yes'. I believed momentum was the same as progress. I didn't realise that true success would eventually mean something quieter. Stability. Peace. The ability to breathe between projects and trust that everything was working as it should.

By this point, you've built something real. You have registered your CIC, found your footing, learned to apply for funding, and maybe even delivered a contract. You have created something that changes lives. Now comes the question that every founder eventually faces: how do you make it last?

Sustainability is not about scraping through or surviving another year. It is about thriving. It is the shift from chasing opportunities to building a structure that stands on its own. It is knowing that your work can continue, even if you need to take a break.

The Three Phases of Growth

Every CIC goes through stages. They might overlap or repeat, but they follow a rhythm that every founder eventually recognises.

Phase One: Survival

You do everything yourself. You rely on small grants, donations and sheer determination. It is exciting and exhausting. This is where you learn fast and adapt constantly.

Phase Two: Stability

You begin to find your flow. Your CIC gains a reputation, you build partnerships, and funding becomes more predictable. You start to think strategically instead of reactively.

Phase Three: Scale

You step back from the daily firefighting and start leading instead of managing. You develop systems, train others and build something that can outlast you.

These phases are not linear. You might move between them many times. The goal is not to rush through them but to recognise where you are and grow intentionally.

What Sustainability Really Means

People often think sustainability means money in the bank. It doesn't. It means resilience.

A sustainable CIC can weather a funding delay, a staff change or a sudden policy shift without collapsing. It has systems that keep the work going even when life throws surprises your way.

Sustainability also means protecting your mission from burnout. It means building a structure that doesn't depend entirely on you. If you have to step away, the work continues. That is real success.

Think of it like building a house. The bricks are your projects, but the foundations are your systems, people and values. Without those, the structure won't last.

Sustainability and Avoiding Burnout

Running a Community Interest Company is deeply rewarding, but it can also be exhausting. You pour your heart, time and energy into helping others, and it is easy to forget to look after yourself in the process. True sustainability is not just about money. It is about time, boundaries and balance.

The beauty of a CIC is its flexibility. You can design your projects around your life, not the other way around. If you know that certain months are busy with family commitments or you want time off during school holidays, plan your projects so that they naturally pause during those times. The freedom to create your own rhythm is one of the greatest advantages of this structure.

Some people choose to take a few weeks or even months off each year between projects. This can be done by planning delivery seasons – for example, running projects from January to June, taking the summer to rest and reflect, and then starting again in autumn. It allows you to sustain your energy and stay creative without burning out.

If you ever need to take unexpected time off due to illness or personal reasons, the CIC model can still work. You can bring in another facilitator or project lead to deliver on your behalf, using your grant funding to cover their costs. Funders understand that life happens. As long as you communicate clearly and have a plan, they are usually supportive.

Burnout often comes from trying to do everything alone. Many CIC founders are perfectionists and people-pleasers. They care deeply, but that same care can become a burden. Building a small team or network around you can make all the difference. Volunteers, freelancers and partner organisations can share the load, and your CIC will grow stronger for it.

Long-term success in community work comes from care that is both outward and inward. You cannot pour from an empty cup. Keep filling yours.

The Shift from Short-Term to Long-Term Thinking

When you start out, every decision feels urgent. You chase the next deadline, the next funder, the next event. That hustle gets you moving, but it can't sustain you forever.

At some point, you must zoom out. Ask yourself, "Where do I want this to be in five years?" The answer doesn't have to be grand. It just needs to be clear.

Short-term thinking is about activity. Long-term thinking is about impact. The most effective CICs know that real change happens when you pace yourself for the marathon, not the sprint.

Diversifying Your Income

The healthiest CICs draw from several income streams. That way, if one slows down, another can carry you.

The main sources are:

- Grants – for innovation and community projects.
- Contracts and commissions – for stability and scale.
- Fundraising – for flexibility and local engagement.
- Trading – for independence and growth.

Balance matters. A good starting point is a 60/40 mix between grants and trading or contracts. Over time, that ratio can shift as your confidence and capacity grow.

Always separate restricted and unrestricted income. Restricted income must be used exactly as agreed with the funder. Unrestricted income is yours to allocate where it is most needed. The latter is your safety net. Even small amounts of unrestricted income – from sales, events or local sponsorship – give you breathing space and creative freedom.

Financial sustainability is just as vital. Relying solely on grant funding can create instability because grants eventually end. The key is to mix your income sources. A sustainable CIC usually has three streams of income: grants, trading and donations.

Grants help you deliver community projects. Trading – such as offering paid workshops, consultancy or selling products – brings in a steady flow of money between projects. Donations and fundraising fill the smaller gaps and will keep the lights on.

You can also build resilience through digital tools that make everyday income easier. One simple and effective example is Easy Fundraising, an online platform that donates a small percentage of online shopping purchases to your chosen CIC. Once set up, it can quietly cover your basic running costs – the sort of small but regular payments that save you from dipping into your own pocket.

When you combine regular income, planned projects and healthy rest periods, you create stability. That stability allows your work to last.

If you want to reduce financial stress even further, think about how your skills can be used for contracts in the future. Councils, schools and local authorities often prefer to work with CICs rather than private businesses because they know that your profits go back into the community. Paid contracts for services like training, wellbeing sessions or creative workshops are an excellent way to diversify your income.

Passive Income Streams

I am passionate about building passive income into your business. Examples include: print-on-demand clothing and merchandise, eBooks, online courses, affiliate income and digital assets. These can be very easy to set up.

Affiliate income, like Easy Fundraising, is where you have a link, people buy something through that link, and you get the commission. In my CIC, I use affiliate links for Amazon items I recommend, insurance I recommend and others. These provide over £1000 into my CIC each month.

Online courses are amazing for passive income and impact. You can make a £99 online course, and just sell it on repeat. I sell around £4k each month of one online course. I use Meta paid ads on Facebook and Instagram to promote and sell on auto.

Print-on-demand is a great way to sell merchandise and clothing without having to buy stock. You can set it up free on sites like Printful. Connect to your Wix website and boom, you're in business. Just upload your designs and get promoted.

This income is well worth the effort of setting it up, as it gives you income with no long-term work. It can tie in with your mission in many ways and help your community.

Online Group Memberships

I am a big advocate of online paid membership for CICs. It can seem tricky when you are giving so much of your service away for free. Make it clear that you have a free level for low-income people or those in need, which is grant-funded or paid for by income generated. Then have a paid membership that gives a different level of service. Online can mean you can reach a wider group of people. A membership can have resources that will sit online in a members-only area. They will typically have online or even in-person group events. Offer pathways to learning or development with clear goals to ensure people stay long-term.

I typically make £1k per month on a simple online membership. I know CICs and limited company social enterprises with £20k memberships.

To set up, follow these steps:

1. Create a lead generation freebie download PDF.
2. Grow an email list and following.
3. Put ads on Meta ads.
4. Create the content and start the online events.
5. Run a launch to drive people in. Make an irresistible offer with a deadline to increase sales drastically.

Managing Multiple Income Streams

Diversification brings stability, but it also brings complexity. You need systems to keep track of it all.

Create a simple cash-flow forecast to plan income and expenses over twelve months. Add a note about when grants are due, when contracts pay, and when you expect fundraising peaks. This will help you avoid gaps between income sources.

Whenever possible, aim to build a small reserve fund. Even one month's operating costs can make all the difference when payments are delayed.

I have, in the early CIC days, had a panic when my grant project ended, as there is always a gap before you can get the next one. My wedding fair income saved me in these times. Having that income was absolutely essential. Later, I developed income strategies so that grants were a bonus, not the core income. Now, my current CIC runs at £90% self-funded. We fund ourselves with fundraising, paid workshops, mural commissions and selling art materials in our shop. Plus, I have developed quality online digital products like eBooks, an online membership and online courses that bring in a tremendous chunk with no effort.

Money doesn't create peace of mind. Systems do.

Trading as a Social Enterprise

Trading income transforms a CIC from fragile to fearless. This is how you earn money while staying true to your mission.

Trading can take many forms. You might sell products, charge for workshops, deliver consultancy or offer creative services. The key is that your trade complements your purpose. An arts CIC might sell prints or host paid exhibitions. A wellbeing CIC could run paid retreats or online courses. An environmental CIC might sell sustainable products or corporate workshops.

Trading teaches you valuable skills such as pricing, marketing and customer relationships. It also shows the world that your work has measurable value.

If you struggle with the idea of charging, remember that being paid for your impact doesn't make it less meaningful. It makes it more sustainable.

Long-Term Planning and Vision

Sustainability is not a reaction: it is a decision. A five-year vision doesn't need to be perfect or corporate. It simply gives direction.

Write down:

- What you want to achieve in five years.
- How many people you'd like to reach.
- What balance you want between funding and trading.
- What kind of team you'll need.
- What impact you can measure to show that you've succeeded.

Revisit it annually. Adjust it as you grow.

Partnerships and Collaboration

No CIC thrives alone. Partnerships multiply impact and open doors that solo work never could. Look for alignment rather than competition. If another organisation is doing similar work, explore collaboration. You might share venues, resources or audiences.

Partnerships also bring credibility. Funders love collaboration because it shows maturity and community focus. One CIC I mentored focused on sports for young people. Another worked on youth mentoring. When they joined forces, they delivered a combined programme that secured a £150,000 contract neither could have achieved alone.

Relationships take time. Send updates even when you don't need anything. Attend events. Offer help. Trust grows quietly, but once it forms, it changes everything.

Building a Team That Can Grow With You

Most founders start out as a one-person army. That is fine at first, but growth demands support.

Hiring doesn't have to mean big payrolls. It could start with a part-time administrator, a freelance designer or a sessional facilitator. The goal is to free your time for the work that only you can do.

As you bring people in, prioritise clarity. Everyone should know their role, their purpose and how their work contributes to the mission.

Leadership isn't about control. It is about creating a space where others can succeed.

Succession planning matters too. Eventually, you'll want your CIC to operate confidently without you in every decision. That is not a loss of control. That is legacy.

Building Systems and Structure

Structure doesn't limit creativity; it protects it.

Set up clear systems for finance, evaluation, communication and safeguarding. Use software that keeps everything organised. Tools like Trello for project management or Xero for accounting can save hours each week.

Good systems reduce chaos. They also build confidence. Funders and commissioners can see instantly when an organisation runs professionally. That trust translates into opportunity.

Even a simple shared folder for policies, reports and templates will make your life easier. Every strong CIC has invisible scaffolding behind the scenes.

The Human Side of Sustainability

At some point, every founder burns out. It often happens quietly, when the adrenaline fades after the busiest period. You stop sleeping properly. You lose joy in the work you love. You start resenting the very thing you built.

I know this because I've been there. There was a time I answered emails at midnight, worked every weekend and believed rest was a luxury. Eventually, I crashed.

That moment taught me a lesson that no grant application ever could. Sustainability is not just financial. It is personal. It is a promise to yourself that you will last long enough to enjoy what you are building.

True sustainability begins when you realise that you are part of the organisation's ecosystem, not its engine. Set boundaries. Take breaks. Celebrate small wins. If you burn out, your CIC suffers too.

The most successful CIC founders know when to pause, when to say no, and when to ask for help. They do not run themselves into the ground trying to be everything to everyone. They recognise that consistency matters more than speed.

So take time to celebrate your wins, no matter how small. Reflect on how far you have come. You are building something that helps people, and that is extraordinary.

Adapting to Change

Adaptability is the secret ingredient of every long-lasting CIC. No matter how well you plan, things will change. Policies shift. Funding priorities move. Communities evolve.

When COVID hit, hundreds of organisations had to reinvent themselves overnight. Some paused. Others adapted. The ones who survived were those who stayed close to their communities, listened to new needs, and found creative ways to deliver.

Change is not failure. It is growth in disguise. Keep your purpose steady, but let your methods evolve.

Measuring and Communicating Impact

As your CIC matures, evidence becomes your most valuable asset. Funders, partners and the public all want to know what difference you make.

Keep evaluation simple and consistent. Collect feedback forms. Record numbers served, outcomes achieved and testimonials. Save photos and case studies as you go.

Share your results proudly. Post them online, email them to partners and include them in funding applications. The more clearly you communicate your success, the more trust you build.

Once a year, create an impact summary. It doesn't have to be a formal report. A few pages of highlights and stories can do wonders for your credibility. Impact is your currency. It tells the world that what you do works.

Resilience and the Founder's Journey

There is a quiet strength in every founder who has lasted beyond the first few years. They've faced rejection, exhaustion and doubt, yet they're still here.

You will meet people who give up after the first major setback. They never get to the point where momentum takes over. But if you hold on through the hard patches, something extraordinary happens. You become resilient.

That resilience doesn't come from winning grants or praise. It comes from persistence. From choosing to keep going even when it feels like no one's watching.

That builds legacy.

The Power of Succession and Legacy

At some stage, your focus will shift from starting your CIC to protecting what you've built. You will begin to think about how your work can continue without you.

This is the ultimate sign of maturity. It is not about stepping away; it's about setting up systems, people and culture that outlast your direct involvement. You might train new leaders, create a trustee board or write down your processes. You might mentor others to start their own CICs.

Legacy doesn't mean leaving. It means letting go enough for the mission to grow beyond you.

My Own Lesson in Longevity

When I started my first CIC, I was juggling delivery, paperwork and fear all at once. I thought success meant staying busy. But then I hit a wall. Funding paused. Projects ended. I suddenly realised that I had built something powerful but fragile.

That moment forced me to rebuild with structure and strategy. I diversified my income, formed partnerships and invested in people. Slowly, the chaos settled into clarity.

Now, when I see founders beginning their journey, I can tell who will make it long term, and they are not the loudest or the most polished. They are the ones who learn how to last.

The Future of the CIC Movement

Community Interest Companies are still young in the grand scheme of things. They represent the best of both worlds – the heart of a charity with the strength of a business.

In the next decade, I believe CICs will become even more central to the UK's social fabric. Imagine every town filled with thriving CICs delivering arts programmes, health projects, education initiatives and environmental solutions.

Imagine if CICs sat at every decision-making table – influencing how councils spend their budgets, how schools support wellbeing, and how NHS trusts design preventative care.

That future isn't far away. It is being built right now, project by project, founder by founder.

Bringing It All Together

Everything you've learned throughout this book – about structure, funding, community, contracts and resilience – comes down to one thing: creating lasting impact.

You don't need to have all the answers. You just need to keep showing up. Keep learning. Keep aligning your work with your purpose.

Your CIC isn't just a business. It is a living reflection of your belief that change is possible.

Sustainability isn't a finish line. It is a mindset. It is the decision to build something that continues to serve long after you've stepped back.

Take a breath and look at how far you've come. You have already done the hardest part – starting. The rest is refinement, growth and persistence.

Your Sustainability Toolkit

CIC Tribe membership has everything you need to grow your CIC. All the pathways in this book are covered. We aim to grow, not burn out. With our easy step-by-step systems, you will be able to really establish your dream CIC and become the social entrepreneur you want to be. Go to **www.kexx.co.uk/membership**

If you are looking to set up your CIC from scratch, use this step-by-step online course for £99, used by over one thousand CICs. We guide you right through the forms for Companies House and show you how to fill in the first grant application, avoiding the mistakes likely to lead to rejection. It is a massive time saver and stress reduction resource: **www.kexx.co.uk/ciccourse**

Final Thoughts

Community Interest Companies are redefining what business looks like. They prove that making a difference and making a living are not opposites.

Whether your CIC serves fifty people a year or five thousand, its value is immeasurable. You are part of a growing movement that is changing lives from the ground up.

Keep going. Keep believing. Keep building with heart and intention. Your story doesn't end with this book. It begins with it.

Reflection:

What is your dream? Think about year-by-year goals for the first three years. How do you want to use this to launch your social enterprise career?

Exercise:

List the key activities your CIC will focus on as it grows. These could include:

- **Developing long-term programmes** that run annually or seasonally, rather than one-off sessions.
- **Building local partnerships** with schools, councils, charities or health organisations to expand your reach.
- **Creating paid services or training packages** that generate steady, unrestricted income.
- **Launching specialised community projects** shaped by participant feedback and emerging needs.
- **Designing digital resources** (online courses, toolkits, webinars) that widen access beyond your local area.
- **Strengthening volunteer and staff pathways**, including training, mentoring and progression opportunities.
- **Running evaluation and impact cycles** to collect stories, data and evidence that support future funding.
- **Exploring new delivery models**, such as outreach, hybrid delivery, mobile provision or satellite hubs.

Choose the activities that feel achievable now, while still creating space for your CIC to evolve.

11

Legacy and the Future of Community Work

By the time you reach this point, you'll have done something most people never manage – moved from an idea to a plan, from intention to structure, from talking about change to building it. You have started something real.

When I look back at my own journey, that first step still feels like the hardest one. I didn't know what I was building or how far it could go. I just knew that something needed to change, and that waiting for someone else to fix it wasn't an option. If that sounds familiar, you're already part of the movement that's reshaping how community work happens in this country.

Community Interest Companies have grown into something much bigger than anyone imagined when the model was first created. They have become the bridge between compassion and professionalism, a space where people with lived experience can build real, lasting impact. What started as a simple legal structure has turned into a national force for good, and it's still growing.

The world around us is changing fast. The last few years have shown us how fragile traditional systems can be and how powerful communities become when they take things into their own hands. CICs sit right at the heart of that shift. They make it possible for people to step up, organise and make things happen. That is not theory. It is happening right now in every town and city across the UK.

I see it every week through CIC Tribe. New founders, new ideas, new ways of tackling the same old problems. It never gets old watching people realise that they have permission to act, and that they can build something that reflects their values and helps others. It is not always easy, but it's always worth it.

Building Legacy in a Changing World

Every chapter in this book has been about building something that lasts – not just a business or a project, but a ripple of change that travels far beyond you. Legacy is not about being remembered. It is about what continues because of you.

The world is changing quickly. We are stepping further into a digital age where screens dominate our days, artificial intelligence is reshaping work, and many people feel more disconnected than ever before. In that kind of world, human contact becomes the most valuable thing we have.

That is where Community Interest Companies come in. They bring people back together. They offer space for connection, creativity and care at a time when both are in short supply. Whether it's a walking group, an art class or a community garden, the future will need these spaces more than ever.

CICs are perfectly positioned for this next chapter. They can adapt to what's happening in the world – to new technologies, new challenges and new opportunities – while keeping people at the centre. As artificial intelligence becomes more common and everyday tasks become automated, our communities will need what machines cannot give: empathy, purpose and belonging.

At the same time, public services continue to shrink. Funding cuts and service closures mean that more responsibility is being handed to community projects and grassroots organisations. While this can feel daunting, it also means that there is more opportunity than ever for CICs to lead the way. Funders and councils are increasingly looking to local groups who understand their communities from the inside. They know that real change happens at kitchen tables, church halls and community centres, not in boardrooms.

We are also seeing a shift in what people value. After years of hustle culture and online noise, more people are craving slower, more meaningful work. They want to make a difference, not just an income. As a result, the CIC movement is growing fast. It offers a model that combines purpose with practicality, giving people the chance to earn fairly while doing good.

The Ripple of Impact

The work you do now lays the foundation for the next generation. Whether you realise it or not, you're shaping a legacy. You might not have thought about it that way yet, but every CIC has a ripple effect. When you deliver a project that changes one person's outlook, that ripple spreads to their family, their friends and their wider community. When you train a volunteer, support a young person or collaborate with another organisation, you're building something that lasts beyond your involvement.

Legacy doesn't have to mean a building or a brand that lives forever. It can simply be the change you've inspired – the people who have found hope because you made a start, the founders who will follow in your footsteps because you showed them it was possible.

Once you begin, the impact multiplies in ways you'll never fully see. That's the beauty of this work.

Sustainability and legacy go hand in hand. The more stable your CIC becomes, the more space you create for others to grow around you. That might mean mentoring new founders, sharing your learning or collaborating with projects that complement your own. The people coming up behind you will need the same encouragement and honesty that you once needed. Offer it freely. That way, this sector keeps its strength.

Mentorship and the Power of Shared Experience

When I first began teaching people how to set up CICs, I thought my work was about forms and funding. Over time, I realised it was really about belief. Every person I've worked with has faced the same doubts: Who am I to do this? What if I fail? What if no one listens?

The truth is, those doubts never disappear completely, but the more you take action, the quieter they become. And that confidence is something you can pass on.

That is why I believe mentorship is one of the most powerful legacies you can leave. The knowledge and experience you share will outlive any project. If everyone who learned something from this book went on to help one other person, the collective impact would be extraordinary.

As you grow, keep looking for ways to support others in the same space. If you've not already, consider joining the CIC Tribe community – a space where founders come together for live sessions, advice and mutual support. It is where you can talk openly about the things that no one else quite understands – the stress, the self-doubt, the small triumphs that mean everything. Having that network behind you can stop you from slipping into what I call 'founder burnout', the exhaustion that comes from carrying everything alone.

In the end, the real legacy of this work is not a company name or a project report. It is the people who were changed by what you built. The young person who found confidence through your workshop. The parent who made a friend at your event. The volunteer who discovered their purpose again.

Technology, Connection and the Future

The sector itself is evolving too. The rise of digital technology has changed how communities connect, fundraise and collaborate. CICs are no longer limited by geography. A founder in Manchester can support someone in Glasgow or Belfast without leaving their living room. Online communities are building their own versions of neighbourhoods, and that opens new opportunities for reach and partnership.

But even as the landscape shifts, the heart of community work remains the same. People still need to feel seen, supported and part of something bigger than themselves. Technology can help us reach further, but real change still happens through human connection. CICs do that better than almost any other model.

The future of this movement belongs to those who can balance purpose with adaptability – the founders who stay close to their communities, listen to what's needed and find practical ways to deliver it. The ones who collaborate rather than compete. The ones who measure their success not only in numbers but in the stories they help create.

As more people realise the potential of CICs, the sector will continue to grow. Councils, health services, schools and funders are already seeing the difference that well-run social enterprises can make. In time, CICs will be recognised not as alternatives but as essential partners in public life. That is the direction we're heading in, and it's an exciting place to be.

The Human Side of Leadership

You might not see yourself as a leader yet, but you are one. The moment you take responsibility for making something happen, you step into leadership. It doesn't require a title or a team; it starts with intention. Leadership in this world looks like persistence, kindness and the ability to keep going even when things get hard.

If you ever feel disheartened, remember this: every founder you admire started exactly where you are. With uncertainty.

With limited resources. With nothing but an idea and a bit of courage. What made the difference wasn't perfection. It was commitment.

And that's what will make the difference for you, too.

Carrying the Movement Forward

As this book comes to a close, take a moment to look back at how far you've come. You have learned what a CIC is, how to structure it, how to fund it, how to grow it and how to make it sustainable. You have heard real stories, absorbed lessons and built a plan that can carry you forward. That is a lot more than most people ever do.

But this isn't the end. It is the point where learning turns into living.

The next chapter doesn't belong to me, or even to this book. It belongs to you. The conversations you'll start. The people you'll help. The ideas you'll test. The change you'll make.

If you remember only one thing from all of this, let it be that you don't have to have everything figured out to begin. Start where you are, use what you have and trust that clarity comes with action.

The future of community work isn't written by institutions. It is written by people like you. You are part of something real now – something that's growing, evolving and changing lives in quiet, determined ways every single day.

So keep going. Keep learning. Keep building.

Your community is waiting. And you're ready.

Reflection:

- What part of this journey has changed you the most?
- When you imagine your CIC five or ten years from now, what does it look like day to day?
- What would you like your community to say about your work when they talk about it in the future?
- How do you want to feel as a founder - proud, calm, fulfilled, secure?

Exercise:

Take a blank page and draw a circle in the centre. Write your CIC's name inside it. Around that circle, add smaller circles with the words that represent your future - things like *growth*, *community trust*, *stability*, *creativity*, *partnerships*, *balance*.

Once you've finished, look at which words matter most to you. These are your guiding priorities for the years ahead.

Then, write a short paragraph beginning with, "My lasting contribution will be..."

Keep it practical and true to what drives you. This isn't about ego or grand plans. It is about clarity - knowing what you want to build and why it matters.

About the Author

Kexx took a leap of faith, swapping her probation officer job to start a CIC and chase her dream of becoming a community artist. Her mission was to engage hard-to-reach young people through the power of art and music.

Over the years, she has run impactful projects in prisons, schools, research and heritage, even supporting schools in The Gambia. Along the way, she's grown as a social entrepreneur, artist and historian, mastering the art of running grant-funded projects that create meaningful impact.

She has fine-tuned strategies to grow different income streams, allowing her to live a dream life while making a difference. She runs a sustainable CIC that creates income without funding.

Kexx also runs CIC Tribe to help others launch their dream CIC careers and have amazing impact in their communities.

Website:

https://www.kexx.co.uk/

YouTube:

www.youtube.com/@kexx_communityartist

Linktr.ee:

https://linktr.ee/kexx_communityartist

www.ingramcontent.com/pod-product-compliance
Lightning Source LLC
LaVergne TN
LVHW022022051126
851858LV00018B/306/J
* 9 7 8 1 9 1 7 6 2 3 4 0 7 *